MORE PRAISE FOR

We Are Americans, We Are Scouts

What wonderful nuggets of Americanism, citizenship, patriotism, service, and duty to our God and country.

Michael D. Buss,
Assistant Director,
Americanism and Children & Youth Division, The American Legion

David Scott has brought together the man and the birth of a movement whose ideals span the century between their times and ours. Indeed, this is the philosophy that gave rise to the 'greatest generation' and can make each succeeding generation great.

Judge Nathan E. White, Jr.,
President General, 2006–2007,
National Society of the Sons of the American Revolution

David Scott masterfully describes the Scouting way of life and connects it to the ideals of President Theodore Roosevelt, including the stewardship of our country's natural resources. This book demonstrates the need for the timeless values the Boy Scouts of America has to offer and its ability to transform young men into ethical, responsible leaders who understand the importance of serving otḥ *̣*̣ *̣*̣*̣ *̣*̣*̣*̣ *̣try.*

ͷle Pete Sessions,
f Representatives

D1264065

Other Scout-Themed Books
by Red Honor Press

Title in Press

In Our Own Way
Living a Scouting Life through Faith

Forthcoming
Youth and Adult Titles

On My Honor, I Will
THE Blueprint for Integrity-Driven® Leadership

Now I Know That!
101 Fun & Fascinating Things to Explore, Learn, and Share

WE ARE

AMERICANS

WE ARE

SCOUTS

From the Mount Rushmore National Memorial in South Dakota, Theodore Roosevelt looks out from beside the carved faces of George Washington, Thomas Jefferson, and Abraham Lincoln. As the twenty-sixth president of the United States, Roosevelt is regarded as one of the world's most important and influential leaders of the twentieth century. In the foreground is the author's troop en route to the XV World Jamboree held in Alberta, Canada, in 1983.

WE ARE
AMERICANS

★

WE ARE
SCOUTS

THE CHIEF SCOUT CITIZEN
ON BUILDING A SCOUTING WAY OF LIFE

WRITTEN AND EDITED BY
David C. Scott

FOREWORD BY
Tweed Roosevelt

RED HONOR™
PRESS

Dallas, Texas

Published by RED HONOR PRESS
An imprint of PenlandScott Publishers

RED HONOR, RED HONOR PRESS, and colophon are trademarks of
Red Honor Ventures, Ltd.

First Edition 2008
10   9   8   7   6   5   4   3   2

Red Honor Press publications are available at special discounted rates for volume and bulk
purchases, corporate and institutional premiums, promotions, fund-raising, and educational
use. For further information, contact:

RED HONOR PRESS
P.O. Box 166677
Irving, Texas 75016

specialsales@redhonor.com

Printed and bound in the United States of America.
Library of Congress Control Number: 2007939538

ISBN-10: 0-9789-8361-0
ISBN-13: 978-0-9789-8361-1

Foreword © 2008 by Tweed Roosevelt.
Cover photograph of President Theodore Roosevelt, © Brown Brothers,
Sterling, Pennsylvania.
Cover photograph of Boy Scouts courtesy of the Harvard College Library,
Cambridge, Massachusetts.

Book design and layout by *the*BookDesigners   www.bookdesigners.com

Get informed and inspired at
www.redhonorpress.com
www.penlandscott.com

For the eight young patriots in
Den 7 of Circle Ten Council's Pack 585:

*Connor, Nicholas, Zachary, Morgan,
Aiden, Patrick, Romano, and Tristan*

The name of Theodore Roosevelt is a talisman possessing magical powers, renewing our faith in our country and our great Scout movement. It revives our courage, gives purpose to our lives, [and] inspires us with . . . a determination to make living worthwhile.

—DANIEL CARTER BEARD,
NATIONAL SCOUT COMMISSIONER,
BOY SCOUTS OF AMERICA, 1910–1941

Contents

CONTENTS

Note to the Reader

In a few cases, the punctuation and spelling of the quotations were updated for today's audience. A short citation has been used for each quotation in the text. The complete citation is included in the Bibliography. The red inset quotations in each chapter are taken from Roosevelt's letters to Chief Scout Executive James E. West. Excerpts from these letters are located in Appendix B.

Foreword

My great-grandfather, *Theodore Roosevelt,* loved children and enjoyed spending time with his four sons and two daughters and their friends. He did all he could as New York governor and then as president of the United States to help America's youth thrive and achieve their fullest potential. For example, he worked hard to preserve the environment for future generations, he supported legislation to end child labor abuses, and he organized the first-ever White House Conference on Children. Although a little-known fact today, he was a great admirer of the Scouting movement and did much to help the Boy Scouts of America become a major national institution. He had strong ideas about the qualities every American should possess and believed that the Scouting experience had much to offer by helping to shape physically fit, mentally alert, and morally upright parents, citizens, and all-around human beings.

This book, which is also a mini-biography of Theodore Roosevelt, reminds us that the good character and high ideals he exemplified and demanded of others are just as important today as they were in his time. It is also a superb reference source for TR's most effective quotations. This book will help Scouts and their families understand the historical underpinnings and social importance of Scouting. In addition, I hope it will persuade more young people to join the Scouts and to learn more about Theodore Roosevelt.

Men like Theodore Roosevelt are needed more than ever before in our fast-changing and sometimes dangerous world. A Scout, to prepare himself for the future, could do worse than emulate Theodore Roosevelt.

—TWEED ROOSEVELT,
BOSTON, MASSACHUSETTS,
OCTOBER 2008

Introduction

Theodore Roosevelt and Scouting in America

In January 1908, the worldwide Scouting movement began when British Army General Robert Baden-Powell published his landmark book, *Scouting for Boys*, stressing the development of morally strong young people committed to duty and service.[1] An immediate best seller, the book laid out a vision of building good citizenship that would be adopted in countries around the globe by the end of the following decade. In late 1908, President Theodore Roosevelt received an inscribed copy of *Scouting for Boys* from Baden-Powell, who knew what a proponent of duty, service, and a productive life the president was. Commented Roosevelt: "I most cordially sympathize with the methods of the book, but perhaps even more with its purpose."

Yet even before receiving Baden-Powell's book, Roosevelt already was associated with the roots of Scouting in America through his endorsement of the camping programs of Ernest Thompson Seton and Daniel Carter Beard, soon to play integral parts in the founding of the Boy Scouts of America. The famed naturalist John Burroughs wrote Roosevelt in 1906 of a unique "boys' Indian camp" he was invited to attend that past July by Seton, an English-born Canadian artist-naturalist, who called the organization the Woodcraft Indians. "[I was] much impressed with it all," proclaimed Burroughs. "I really think it well worthy of your attention and encouragement." Roosevelt agreed and sent Seton a note of support that was read to a group of Woodcraft campers later that summer.

The following year, Dan Beard, who had earlier founded his own Scout-like organization known as the Sons of Daniel Boone, also sought Roosevelt's endorsement. Like the Woodcraft Indians, the Sons of Daniel Boone strove to build character in the nation's youth through the example of rugged American pioneers, Beard's childhood heroes. During an invited meeting with the president at the White House in 1907, Beard proposed a heroism award named in honor of Roosevelt because of his powerful belief in giving service to others. Upon hearing this, the president gave his approval by exclaiming, "Bully!" and slamming both fists firmly down onto his desk. To Roosevelt, there was no question of the value to the nation of wilderness and ideals-based youth programs such as those established by Seton and Beard.

As the excitement of Baden-Powell's version of Scouting spread from country to country, it was only a matter of time before the United States would join in the organized global phenomenon. By February 1910, the Boy Scouts of America was incorporated in Washington, D.C., by an enterprising Chicago newspaperman named William D. Boyce. By June, the Boy Scouts of America was headquartered in a YMCA building in New York City.

In January 1911, the Executive Board of the Boy Scouts of America hired a Washington lawyer named

James E. West as their first executive secretary (the original title for Chief Scout Executive). West had established a reputation for working with youth, convincing Theodore Roosevelt to host the White House Conference on Children in 1909. Roosevelt told West: "I have always thought well of you, but I now feel that you are one of those [distinguished] and patriotic citizens to whom this country stands under a peculiar debt of gratitude." This appreciation would help West engage Roosevelt on behalf and to the benefit of formal Scouting in America.

At the beginning of the twentieth century, Roosevelt had a concern that traditional codes of honor and chivalry were not being followed or even understood. But his position as president of the United States allowed him to counter those concerns and visibly set a strong, positive example for the nation's youth to follow. He knew that young people needed physical competition to develop their sense of self-worth, and all needed to succeed. Yet success alone would not create good citizen-leaders, meaning honorable and exemplary youth, who would be community role models. Success had to be combined with a sense of strong morals. He saw the Scouting program's emphasis on "doing one's duty" as the solution, along with developing moral power through positive action.

Duty was on the forefront of Roosevelt's belief system—duty to God, duty to country, duty to family, and duty to self—core convictions that "as principles seem to me vital, and from which I shall never deviate," he wrote. When Seton and Beard joined the growing ranks of community supporters of the young Boy Scouts of America in 1910, Roosevelt completed the circle by embracing the Boy Scouts of America's mission and by writing letters of support for its patriotic and civic ideals. Roosevelt saw that the Boy Scouts of America could create better citizen-leaders through strict adherence to its core tenets expressed in the Scout Oath, the Scout Law, the Scout motto: "Be Prepared," the Scout slogan: "Do a Good Turn Daily," and, eventually, the Outdoor Code.

Theodore Roosevelt recognized that all youth could effect change in the community and country through personal action, a commitment to serve others, and through setting a positive example for others to follow, all for the common good. He firmly believed that every person had a responsibility to perform these simple civic duties. The result, he knew, would be a legion of high-quality citizen-leaders who could help their fellow countrymen during challenging times. "I have a great deal of faith in the . . . American citizen," he said.

Roosevelt was offered the newly created post of Chief Scout Citizen in January 1912. He enthusiastically accepted and held this honorary title until his death in January 1919. History has shown that Roosevelt's support of the Boy Scouts of America was a critical factor in the lasting success of the program. His singular endorsement also encouraged other influential men across the nation to lend their own support to the movement that a century later has produced the modern Scouting program we know today. The millions of Scouts and leaders who have embraced the moral principles of Scouting can be thankful for the vision, example, and support of one of America's foremost presidents, Theodore Roosevelt.

—D. C. S.,
DALLAS, TEXAS,
OCTOBER 2008

[The Boy Scouts of America] insists on the doing of a good turn daily to somebody without reward, and thus furnish the elements of a national, widespread courtesy. You stand for true patriotism, true citizenship, true Americanism.

—LETTER FROM ROOSEVELT TO JAMES E. WEST,
FEBRUARY 10, 1911

About This Book

We Are Americans, We Are Scouts celebrates the timeless values of Scouting as seen through Theodore Roosevelt's wisdom and words. The stories and quotations that follow are relevant wherever a quotation or anecdote is required to inspire an audience on themes of values, character, and patriotism. It will also help Scouts make good decisions at meaningful points in their lives. It is a portable reference book for Scouts, leaders, speakers, parents, and mentors trying to assert and reinforce the value of living an honorable, worthy life, as well as for those "teaching moments" so fundamental to Scouting.

To provide a readily accessible source of inspiration, We Are Americans, We Are Scouts is organized according to the founding tenets of Scouting.

Readers of We Are Americans, We Are Scouts can achieve a fuller understanding of the fundamental values of our common Scouting heritage through the inspiring words and stories of Theodore Roosevelt, a man of public service and duty who set a powerful moral example for America. Considered by some to be the last Renaissance man to occupy the White House, Roosevelt's vast intellect and unshakable moral fortitude enabled him to show America the way to national improvement at a critical point in its history.

As an outstanding example of cheerful and dutiful service to others, and a national icon who believed Scouting to be important to all Americans, Theodore Roosevelt's spirit and message continues to remind us that virtue and noble character are the keys to a fulfilling life.

CHAPTER ONE

The Scout Oath

Roosevelt speaking at Evanston, Illinois, in April 1903.

The Scout Oath

The origins of the Scout Oath date back to 1903 when Robert Baden-Powell, the founder of the world-wide Scouting movement, was still an active army general.[1] In an address to his soldiers, he advised them to keep improving themselves, to avoid doing anything "low or underhanded" that would undermine their self-respect, and to always be guided by a sense of duty about what is right rather than what is easiest. By 1911, the Scout Oath had evolved into the version that every member of the Boy Scouts of America has pledged for the past century:

> *On my honor I will do my best*
> *To do my duty to God and my country*
> *and to obey the Scout Law;*
> *To help other people at all times;*
> *To keep myself physically strong,*
> *mentally awake, and morally straight.*

The Oath of the Boy Scouts of America envisions a life spent doing one's duty to God, country, family, and self. Its opening line states, "On my honor I will do my best." The Oath does not say, "I will *try* to do my best," or "I *hope* to do my best." It says, "I *will* do my best." There's a big difference.

Throughout his life of public service, Theodore Roosevelt did not merely *try* to do his best—he *did* his best. He was a national leader, a dedicated husband and father to six children, and a friend to many; and in all his roles, he always did his best.

Right up until his death in 1919, he stayed especially true to the last part of the Oath—the pledge to keep "physically strong, mentally awake, and morally straight." Roosevelt also believed that people who lack a strong sense of duty to God, country, or self cannot do their best to keep their country great.

Roosevelt paid a great deal of attention to one important, unstated aspect of the Oath: citizenship. He believed being a good citizen gave meaning to life, going so far as to say that "unless its prime aim [is] the doing of duty," the life of a person has little meaning at all.

In Roosevelt's own life, the call to duty and citizenship took many forms. For years before the start of the Spanish-American War, Roosevelt had dreamed of leading a team of soldiers—a group of "harum-scarum riders," as he put it—on horseback during a battle. He joined the First U.S. Volunteer Cavalry Regiment after the war began in 1898. By mid-June of that year, he was deployed to Cuba as a lieutenant-colonel, leading exactly the kind of military unit he'd imagined.

On July 1, 1898, in the heat of battle beneath Kettle Heights and San Juan Hill, Roosevelt led his men in a dangerous charge across an open valley as bullets rained down from defensive positions. Roosevelt's Rough Riders, as they came to be known, were strengthened by his leadership and bravery.

Just over a century later, in 2001, President William J. Clinton awarded

EVERY HEALTHY [SCOUT] OUGHT TO FEEL IT IS NECESSARY TO HAVE A CONSTRUCTIVE NATURE.

Roosevelt posthumously the Congressional Medal of Honor, the nation's highest military award to men and women. It was received by Roosevelt's great-grandson, Tweed Roosevelt. This medal further confirmed, so many years later, that as a soldier, president, and family man, Roosevelt did his best to live the principles ingrained in the Scout Oath.

DUTY TO GOD

Theodore Roosevelt believed that a strong faith in God was the first step toward good citizenship.[2] He didn't care about a person's faith tradition as long as they respected a supreme creator. "The nation that in actual practice [loves] God," Roosevelt said, "is the nation which does not wrong its neighbors." Roosevelt understood that faith in God gave people a reliable moral compass to consult in times of difficulty or temptation. He often spoke about God as the source of righteousness.

In November 1917, Roosevelt visited Camp Upton in Long Island, New York. Camp Upton was a training facility for army recruits during the early stages of the U.S. involvement in World War I. During the visit, Roosevelt delivered two inspirational speeches to the soldiers, known then as "doughboys," to hearten them in their battle overseas. He brought with him hundreds of special copies of the New Testament of the Holy Bible to give to the men. Each Bible had been printed with a dedication written by Roosevelt himself quoting scripture. The dedication read in part: "What doth the Lord require of thee than to do justice, and to love mercy, and to walk humbly with thy God."

For Roosevelt, these words conveyed the essence of faith. The quotations that follow help us understand what religion meant to Roosevelt and how it intertwined with citizenship:

When faith is strong and belief very sincere,
[a Scout] must possess great wisdom, broad charity,
and the ability to learn by experience.

— Roosevelt's *Oliver Cromwell* [3]

The religious [person] is . . . the [person]
whose religion bids [them to] strive to advance
decency and clean living and to make the world a
better place for [their] fellows to live in.

—Address, Cambridge, Massachusetts, February 23, 1907

More and more [people] . . . are learning the
grandest of all lessons — that they can best serve
their God by serving their fellow men.

—Roosevelt's *Oliver Cromwell* [4]

It is . . . important that a people should be of full
stature from the spiritual and moral standpoint.

—"The People of the Pacific Coast," *Outlook*,
September 23, 1911

We must stand . . . against irreverence
in all things of the spirit.

— "The Search for Truth in a Reverent Spirit,"
Outlook, December 2, 1911

DUTY TO COUNTRY

It's not difficult to see that serving his country was Roosevelt's greatest ambition.[5] He wasn't one to let anything stand in the way of his duty to country. Three weeks before the 1912 presidential election, he arrived to speak in Milwaukee, Wisconsin, to talk about how well his political party was doing to improve the lives of average Americans. However, while getting out of his car, Roosevelt was shot in the chest by a would-be assassin. Fortunately, he survived because the bullet was slowed by the thick, folded speech and an eyeglass case in his breast pocket. But instead of canceling the event and allowing doctors to examine him, five minutes later Roosevelt shocked the audience by taking the stage and making that speech! Yet now his speech had a much greater importance.

He was not angry or scared that day, he was a proud American who was trying to make his country better through his positive attitude and strong example.

"I have a message to deliver, and I will deliver it as long as there is life in my body," he declared to the delighted audience. "I am very much uninterested in whether I am shot or not. I am not thinking of my life or of anything connected with me personally. I am thinking of the movement . . . a [political] movement to try to take the burdens off the men and especially the women and children of this country."

When he finally allowed doctors to examine him, they found the bullet lodged deeply in his chest. Because it didn't seem to pose a threat to his health, it was never removed. "I had to make that speech!" he later told a friend. "If I were to die, I especially wished to make the speech; if I were to recover, I might as well make it."

The quotations that follow underscore the incredible sense of duty to America that made Roosevelt's actions not only possible but the *only* possible course of action:

Love of country is an elemental virtue.

—*American Ideals and Other Essays*[6]

Patriotism means service to the nation.

—Address, Lincoln, Nebraska, June 14, 1917

Patriotism should be an integral part of our every feeling at all times.

—*Fear God and Take Your Own Part*[7]

I ask that [Americans] rise level to the greatness of opportunities.

—*The Americanism of Theodore Roosevelt*[8]

*Any deed that reflects credit on the American
name is a subject of congratulations for every
American of every section of this country.*

—Address, Chicago, Illinois, April 29, 1916

*Americanism is not a matter of creed or birthplace
or descent. The best American . . . has in [them] the
American spirit, the American soul.*

—Address, New York City, New York, March 17, 1905

DUTY TO SELF

At certain times in our lives, we all have to set aside time for ourselves.[9] We tend to do this after a stressful or very emotional period in our lives. For Roosevelt, this time came in 1884 when his wife and his mother died in the same house, both on Valentine's Day.

Roosevelt's response to this double loss was to emotionally regroup by moving to the West for a spell to regain his focus and zest for life. In what was called at that time the Dakota Territory, Roosevelt took up a brief ranching career that let him reconnect with his love for nature and hard work. He faced many difficulties in the Badlands that he didn't face in city life, such as dealing with the unpredictable outside elements and living without indoor plumbing. He had to depend on his own physical strength and mental discipline to survive.

Roosevelt's time in the West helped him reflect on his life's goals. The experience helped transform him into the fearless, morally straight, devoted public servant who would go on to become the twenty-sixth president of the United States.

His duty to self is reflected in the following quotations:

We are honor bound to put into practice what we preach.

—"Latitude and Longitude among Reformers,"
Century Magazine, June 1900

A ton of talk weighs less than nothing, if . . . not backed by action.

—*Theodore Roosevelt: His Life and Work* [10]

Nothing worth gaining is ever gained without effort.

—*American Ideals and Other Essays* [11]

It is a good thing to be a good half-back, but it is a mighty bad thing if at forty all you can say of a [person] is that [they were] a good half-back.

—*Strenuous Epigrams of Theodore Roosevelt* [12]

[Scouts] . . . must rely upon [themselves].
[They] must take pride in [their] own work,
instead of sitting idle to envy the luck of others.

— "How Not to Better Social Conditions,"
Review of Reviews, January 1897

Keep your eyes on the stars, but remember
to keep your feet on the ground.

— *The Strenuous Life* [13]

Do not let play interfere with work.

— "The American Boy," *St. Nicholas*, May 1900

Let us strive for success, even if
by doing so we risk failure.

— Address, Oxford, England, June 7, 1910

PHYSICALLY STRONG

As a boy, Roosevelt had poor eyesight and suffered so severely from asthma that he had to sleep propped up on pillows or in a chair.[14] His father encouraged him not to let these physical difficulties hold him back. By working out every day, such as lifting weights, swimming, hiking, and riding horseback, he was able to live a full life. He learned wrestling, boxing, and judo, and enjoyed playing sports as much as he enjoyed watching them.

While still president in January 1909, Roosevelt heard that many cavalry officers had been complaining about the army's rigorous fitness standards, which required that they be able to ride 100 miles in three days. To set an example (and to stop them from whining), the forty-nine-year-old Roosevelt got on his horse in the early morning before daybreak and rode one hundred miles in seventeen hours from the White House to Warrenton, Virginia, and back again in the winter cold. He could not have performed this feat had he not been in excellent physical shape.

Although a healthy man, Roosevelt had experienced many mishaps during his lifetime. He had been thrown by a bronco at his ranch and broken three ribs. He attempted to ford the Little Missouri River and almost died in quicksand. One time, he and his horse tumbled down a hundred-foot embankment, a mishap from which he emerged with deep bruises. He carried a scar received while fencing. He bore another scar on his left shoulder from being mauled by a grizzly bear. He was wounded by bomb shrapnel in the assault on San Juan Hill. He was badly bruised in a trolley car crash and carried a bullet in his chest from a would-be assassin. In spite of all this, Roosevelt preached and practiced exercise and sport, which he fervently believed helped him survive these accidents, as well as his youthful physical challenges, to make him a better citizen-leader.

"I have fought and not always won," he once said. "But I can say that I always came up for the next fight when I lost."

He frequently wrote about his views on physical exercise and keeping one's body strong:

We must all either wear out or rust out,
every one of us. My choice is to wear out.

—*Strenuous Epigrams of Theodore Roosevelt* [15]

Our object is to get as many of our people as possible to take part in . . . healthy, vigorous pastimes, which will benefit the whole nation.

—"Professionalism in Sports," *North American Review*, August 1890

Do not [let sports] degenerate into the sole end of anyone's existence.

—Letter to his son Kermit Roosevelt, October 4, 1903

To work hard at a sport which entails severe physical exertion and steady training also implies character.

—"Character and Success," *Outlook*, March 31, 1900

MENTALLY AWAKE

What many people remember most about Roosevelt to-day is that he was a president, a conservationist, and a Rough Rider who won the battle of San Juan Hill.[16] Not everyone realizes that he was also an intellectual, which means he read a great deal, wrote a great deal, and asked many questions. He was curious and constantly learning. He published his first scholarly book at twenty-three years of age when he was still in law school. He was fluent in French and German. Roosevelt kept his mind sharp by trying to learn something new every day.

Reading was one of Roosevelt's greatest passions. While president, he always took a book to read in the executive office in spare moments. After his presidential term ended in early 1909, Roosevelt left for Africa to collect animal specimens for the Smithsonian Institution. He brought with him some of the world's greatest books by Mark Twain, Charles Dickens, Sir Walter Scott, and Alfred Lord Tennyson, among others. The collection became known as Roosevelt's "Pigskin Library" because all the volumes were bound in hog's hide.

"They were for use, not ornament," Roosevelt said of his portable library. "I almost always had some volume with me." He would read in his spare time or while waiting for camp to be made. Over time, the books became stained with the "blood, sweat, gun oil, dust, and ashes" he encountered on his travels, which merely made them even more special to him. "With me," Roosevelt later recounted, "reading is a disease."

He often spoke and wrote about the importance of intellectual pursuits:

The greatest doer must also be the great dreamer.

—Address, Berkeley, California, March 23, 1911

The things of the spirit are even more important than the things of the body.

—Address, "The World Movement,"
Berlin, Germany, May 12, 1910

We need intellect and there is no reason why we should not have it together with character.

—*American Ideals and Other Essays* [17]

Intellect is a great thing.

—Address, Tarrytown, New York, October 11, 1897

If [Scouts have] in [them] the right stuff, it is a great advantage to [them] should [their] circumstances be so fortunate as to enable [them] to get the years of additional mental training.

—"Character and Success," *Outlook*, March 31, 1900

MORALLY STRAIGHT

When President William McKinley was assassinated in 1901, Vice President Theodore Roosevelt was to be sworn in as president of the United States.[18] He arrived in Buffalo, New York, to meet with McKinley's advisors. Secretary of War Elihu Root asked Roosevelt to take the oath of office.

When it was time, Roosevelt stood in front of the advisors and gave the shortest inauguration speech in history. "I shall take the oath at once," he said, "and in this hour of deep and terrible national bereavement I wish to state that it shall be my aim to continue absolutely unbroken the policy of President McKinley for the peace and prosperity and honor of our beloved country."

One observer concluded that Roosevelt's brief but powerful statement "solved the political and commercial crisis" caused by McKinley's assassination. It was clear from the beginning, to all who heard him speak, that Roosevelt had strong moral principles, and would be true to them as president.

His words and writings reinforced his strong moral commitments:

There can be no compromise on the great fundamental principles of morality.

—"The Best and the Good," *Churchman*, March 17, 1900

If courage and strength and intellect are unaccompanied by the moral purpose—the moral sense — they become merely forms of expression for unscrupulous force and unscrupulous cunning.

—Address, Colorado Springs, Colorado, August 2, 1901

The worst ill that can befall us is to have our own souls corrupted.

—*Realizable Ideals*[19]

Wrongs should be strenuously and fearlessly denounced.

—"College and Public Life," *Atlantic Monthly*, August 1894

We cannot be dragged up. We have got to push ourselves up.

—*Strenuous Epigrams of Theodore Roosevelt*[20]

What we need is a sufficient number of [citizen-leaders] who can work well and who will work with a high ideal.

—Address, Groton, Massachusetts, May 24, 1904

CHAPTER TWO

The Scout Law

Roosevelt preparing to ride through Yellowstone National Park in April 1903.

The Scout Law

ike the Scout Oath, the Scout Law has its roots in Robert Baden-Powell's 1903 farewell address to his soldiers, in which he encouraged them to be "helpful and courteous to all."[1] By 1908, the original British Scouting version had nine key values—to which the Boy Scouts of America added "brave," "clean," and "reverent" in 1911—resulting in the twelve points of the Scout Law that we know so well today.

> *A Scout is: Trustworthy,*
> *Loyal,*
> *Helpful,*
> *Friendly,*
> *Courteous,*
> *Kind,*
> *Obedient,*
> *Cheerful,*
> *Thrifty,*
> *Brave,*
> *Clean, and*
> *Reverent*

The Scout Law focuses on what a Scout *should* do, rather than telling a Scout what *not* to do. As one Boy Scouts of America founder noted, it's "do" rather than "don't."

Throughout Roosevelt's writings, the ideals within the Scout Law come up again and again. "The citizenship of any country is worthless unless in a crisis it shows the spirit," he once said. The Scout Law captures the spirit of every good American citizen and on many occasions, Roosevelt lived it.

On New Year's Day 1907, Roosevelt stood in a receiving line in the White House, welcoming every American who stopped by to wish him a Happy New Year. The president looked each visitor in the eye as the endless line of people filed past.

Over the course of four hours, Roosevelt shook over 8,000 hands—an average of almost thirty-five handshakes per minute! He told each visitor that he was delighted to make his or her acquaintance. Roosevelt was so cheerful that one young man who stood in line reported going home to "wring the personality" out of his clothes.

THE MOVEMENT IS ONE FOR PATRIOTISM.

"I enjoy being president," Roosevelt once declared. Surely no one ever had more fun in the job.

TRUSTWORTHINESS

Scouts know that it is not always easy to be honest, even if it is always right.[2] Roosevelt knew this, too, and he valued honesty and trustworthiness in his own children, as well as his friends, and his employees.

During cattle drives at his western ranch, Roosevelt rode and slept alongside the cowboys who worked for him. Back then, cattle ranchers worked on the "open range" system, meaning there were no property fences to keep neighboring animals off of your land. One day on a neighbor's range, he and a cowboy lassoed a young steer that had not been branded. His employee prepared the irons to mark the steer with Roosevelt's brand. Roosevelt pointed out that the steer was on his neighbor's land, and should therefore be branded by his neighbor. "But I always put on the boss's brand," said the cowboy.

"Drop that iron," said Roosevelt, "and get back to the ranch and get out. A man who will steal *for* me will steal *from* me."

Later on in his career he wrote:

You must have honesty as the first
requisite of good citizenship.

—Address, Newburgh, New York, February 28, 1900

If anyone lies . . . you cannot deal with [them]
because there is nothing to depend on.

—*Strenuous Epigrams of Theodore Roosevelt* [3]

We need fearless criticism of dishonest [people] and of
honest [people] on any point where they go wrong.

—"The Eighth and Ninth Commandments in Politics,"
Outlook, May 12, 1900

*We should not take part in acting a lie any
more than in telling a lie.*

—Address, "The Man in the Arena,"
Paris, France, April 23, 1910

The light of day is a great deterrent to wrong-doing.

—*Strenuous Epigrams of Theodore Roosevelt* [4]

LOYALTY

In Roosevelt's time, the president was much more approachable than he is today.[5] Ordinary people could go to the White House on special occasions and stand in line to meet and greet the president. Yet Roosevelt was more readily available to some people than to others. His door was always open to the men who fought alongside him as Rough Riders in the Spanish-American War.

Coming to see the president on one occasion with important business, Senator Shelby M. Cullom of Illinois was told at the door that Roosevelt had been visiting in his office with a former Rough Rider for the past half hour. The legislator grabbed his hat and turned on his heel, saying, "Well, what chance have I, then? I'm only a senator."

Roosevelt's loyalty was well understood and respected, and he often spoke and wrote of it:

*I entirely appreciate loyalty to one's friends, but loyalty
to the cause of justice and honor stands above it.*

—Letter to a Senator from Oregon, May 15, 1905

*Let us be loyal to great ideals. But . . .
unless we show common sense in action, loyalty
in speech will amount to considerably less.*

—*The Great Adventure* [6]

*If the [Scout] is a decent [Scout],
whether well off or not well off, stand by him [or her].*

—Address, Oyster Bay, New York, August 16, 1903

The disloyal [person] . . . is our worst foe.

—*The Great Adventure* [7]

HELPFULNESS

Roosevelt was very fond of giving advice and, knowing
this, citizens sought his help with their businesses, rela-
tionships, and families.[8] Fortunately for them, he was a
wise man with a great deal of wisdom to share.

A friend once asked Roosevelt to talk to his son, whom
the man considered disobedient. Roosevelt agreed to do

so and was surprised to find the young man "clean-cut and upstanding." The boy told Roosevelt that his father was impatient and "explodes every time the least thing not scheduled happens."

After talking to both father and son, Roosevelt determined that the two had difficulty showing respect for one another.

Roosevelt told his friend what he had learned. "All this trouble you've brought on yourself," he told him. "You've been too busy making money to have paid much attention to him [his son]." Instead of advising the son, he ended up advising the father.

Weeks later, the son proclaimed to Roosevelt that his father was a changed man and that their relationship was much improved. "Young man," Roosevelt replied, "all I told him was to get acquainted with you."

Roosevelt would give this same advice to any father and son having difficulty getting along. It is simple but helpful: the better you know a person, the more you can see things from his or her point of view.

His helpfulness was evident from his many writings:

The only permanent way by which an individual can be helped is to help [them] to help [themselves].

—Address, Cairo, Egypt, March 28, 1910

The strong should always be glad of the chance in turn to aid the weak.

—"Civic Helpfulness," *Century Magazine*, October 1900

*If a [person] stumbles, it is a good thing to help
[that person] to [his or her] feet. Every one of us needs
a helping hand now and then.*

—Address, "Man in the Arena," Paris, France, April 23, 1910

*The greatest possible good can be done by the
extension of a helping hand at the right moment,
but the attempt to carry anyone permanently
can end in nothing but harm.*

—"Civic Helpfulness," *Century Magazine,* October 1900

FRIENDLINESS

Roosevelt was a friendly man and genuinely enjoyed meeting people.[9] Although he was the first president to receive the protection of the Secret Service, people were permitted to approach him at his many speeches and addresses.

An elderly woman from Florida once told him that she had come all the way from Jacksonville to Washington to see what a living president looked like. "I never saw one," she told him.

Part of being friendly is being able to put people at ease. "That's very kind of you," Roosevelt told the woman. "Persons from up here go all the way to Florida just to see a live alligator!"

Another time a man went to see Roosevelt at the White House on official business. He went into Roosevelt's office and a half hour later he came out again. "What did you say to him?" a friend asked. The man replied, "All I told him was my name."

To Roosevelt, no man was a stranger, and it didn't take much to engage him in conversation.

Roosevelt's friendliness is evident from his actions and also from his writings and speeches:

The spirit of [fellowship] in American citizenship,
when rightly understood and rightly applied,
is more important than [anything] else.

—Address, Chicago, Illinois, September 3, 1900

[Americans] freely extend the hand of welcome and of
good fellowship to every [person], no matter
what [their] creed or birthplace.

—*American Ideals and Other Essays* [10]

Any healthy-minded American is bound to
think well of [their] fellow Americans if [they]
only get to know them.

—"Fellow-Feeling," *Century Magazine*, June 1900

We need [citizens] who try to be their poorer
brothers' keepers to the extent of befriending them

and working with them so far as they are willing.

> — "Latitude and Longitude among Reformers,"
> *Century Magazine*, June 1900

COURTESY

Roosevelt believed firmly in respecting the dignity of all people, regardless of race or religion.[11] Shortly after becoming president, he invited Booker T. Washington, the most famous African-American at that time, to dine at the White House. It was the first time a person of color had ever eaten a meal at the president's table, a groundbreaking event covered extensively by the media. By early the following morning, the American public knew all about it. Some were pleased, but many were outraged in that era of racial discrimination and segregation.

It was not only courteous of Roosevelt to invite Washington for dinner but also courageous. The event foreshadowed a day when crusaders like Martin Luther King Jr. would work together with political leaders for equality among people of all races.

Roosevelt's fabled courtesy was something he *lived*, though others only discussed it. He often wrote about courtesy and generosity as well:

> *Courtesy is as much the mark of a gentleman*
> *as truthfulness and courage, and every*

American boy should be a gentleman.

—Letter to James E. West, February 10, 1911

It is a mistake to let other people grow selfish.

—*An Autobiography*[12]

Treat all Americans as [if] on the same footing.

—*The Great Adventure*[13]

We need most [of all] to understand the other's viewpoint. . . . That is helpful to your neighbor.

—*Theodore Roosevelt: His Life and Work*[14]

KINDNESS

Being kind is as important for a president as it is for a Scout, and Roosevelt always did his best to be kind to others, especially to those less fortunate.[15]

One day at the White House, Roosevelt was approached by a little boy who had worked his way to the front of a large group of visitors. "What can I do for you?" the president asked him. The boy told him that his father had just died, leaving his mother penniless. The only thing the family owned that was worth anything was a typewriter, which the boy had brought to the White House as a gift to the president. Roosevelt asked the boy to wait for him to finish attending to the other visitors. When that was done, he returned to the boy and sent him off—one typewriter lighter—but with some unexpected money in his pocket.

On another occasion, Roosevelt was on his way to have lunch with two foreign ambassadors when he came across a small boy sobbing in the street. The lad had become separated from his family and was lost in the city. Roosevelt, knowing that he was keeping the ambassadors waiting, took the boy to the local police station and instructed them to put out a citywide alert for his parents. Then he gave the boy some money and left for his appointment. To Roosevelt, a ten-year-old boy was more important than two ambassadors conducting important state business.

Roosevelt's kindness was inherent, but he urged others to show sympathy as well:

Sympathy, in the broadest sense, is the most important factor in producing a healthy . . . life.

—"Fellow-Feeling as a Political Factor,"
Century Magazine, June 1900

*Without sympathy . . .
no permanent good can be accomplished.*

—"Fellow-Feeling as a Political Factor,"
Century Magazine, June 1900

*Goodness and strength must go
hand in hand if the Republic is to be preserved.*

—"Professionalism in Sports,"
North American Review, August 1890

*Fellow-feeling means a realization of
the fundamental equality of all of us in need.*

—"The Church and the People," *Outlook*, January 27, 1912

*Sympathy must be kept close at heart if we are
to do our work well here in our American life.*

—*The Strenuous Life* [16]

OBEDIENCE

Before Roosevelt became president, he spent a lot of time in what is now Medora, North Dakota, where he acquired his conviction about the need to preserve nature.[17] In 1883, he went to the Badlands, an area of rugged terrain in the Dakota Territory, and involved himself in the cattle business.

Like most presidents, Roosevelt considered upholding the law very important. During the time he spent at Elkhorn Ranch, as he called it, he always obeyed and respected the law. He was appointed acting deputy sheriff, and from time to time he arrested bandits and cattle thieves. On one occasion, a bandit gang headed by an unpleasant fellow known as "Bad-Man Finnegan" escaped down the Little Missouri River by stealing Roosevelt's own river boat.

A lesser man might have let them escape, but Roosevelt and two other men quickly lashed some logs together into a makeshift flatbed boat, gathered food and water, then set off in pursuit. They navigated 150 miles before seeing smoke rising from the brush on the riverbank. There were the bandits, sitting in camp. Roosevelt and his men arrested the three criminals, and he alone walked them through the wilderness to the ranch of a friend and then to the nearest jail in the town of Dickinson.

When word of Roosevelt's exploit reached his community, he was considered a hero, not only because he'd pursued the men, but also because under "frontier justice," most peace officers of that time would have immediately punished the bandits instead of making the arduous overland journey to take them in to stand trial. Roosevelt believed laws existed for a reason. On reaching the jail, the scraggly, scratched, and bruised Roosevelt appeared to an observer to be as "gritty and determined as a bulldog."

Roosevelt's dedication to the law helped to distinguish his public service career. He went on to say and write:

No [person] is above the law and no [person] is below it.

—Address, "Third Annual Message to Congress,"
Washington, D.C., December 7, 1903

*We the people must show obedience
to the law, loyalty to our ideals, self-control,
self-mastery, [and] self-restraint.*

—Address, Portsmouth, Rhode Island, July 2, 1913

*When we [ask citizens to] obey the law, we insure for
[them] the absolute protection of the law.*

— "The Trusts and the Tariff," *Outlook*, September 27, 1902

CHEERFULNESS

At the White House during Roosevelt's presidency, dinner was a big event, with many people from different walks of life seated at the dining table, laughing, and telling stories together.[18]

One night, Roosevelt invited a cowboy friend from his ranching days to dine with him and the British ambassador. "Now, Jimmy," the president jokingly told the cow-puncher beforehand, "Don't bring your gun along tonight. The British ambassador is going to dine, too, and it wouldn't do for you to pepper the floor 'round his feet with bullets to see a tenderfoot dance."

A sense of humor pervaded much of what Roosevelt said and wrote:

*Happiness and usefulness are largely
found in the same soul.*

—Address, "A Square Deal," Syracuse,
New York, September 7, 1903

*The greatest happiness is the happiness that comes
as a by-product of striving to do what must be done.*

—*An Autobiography*[19]

*The joy of life is won in its deepest and truest sense
only by those who have not shirked life's burdens.*

—Address, "A Square Deal," Syracuse,
New York, September 7, 1903

*If we couldn't laugh once in a while, what
a world this would be! It wouldn't be
a world—it would be a madhouse.*

—*Talks with TR*[20]

THRIFT

Roosevelt was a practical man who knew how to take an idea and turn it into a reality, once admitting to a friend that he had a "second-rate brain" but "a capacity for action."[21] He learned this from his father. But

Theodore Roosevelt Sr. was less successful in passing on to young Theodore the virtue of thrift. The elder Roosevelt gave his son the very good advice of always spending less than he earned. "Keep the fraction constant," he told Theodore Jr.—that is, make sure any increase in personal spending is in proportion with gains in income.

As an adult, Roosevelt tried to live on a budget and to account for his expenditures, but he was not always successful. His more frugal wife, Edith, imposed on him a personal budget of five dollars a day and made him account for his expenditures. To settle household bills, she wrote out checks and set them down one by one for his signature.

For all of his achievements, Roosevelt had shortcomings, too. But he accepted help from his wife to incorporate the quality of thrift not already present in his life. He had the wisdom to know when he needed help and, further, to accept it.

Writing about thrift, he therefore was able to acknowledge:

All honor [goes] to the [Scout] who [is] on the watch to take advantage of every opportunity to do good with [his or her] money.

—Address, Ithaca, New York, December 29, 1900

It is really less a question of spending more money than of knowing how to get the best results for the money that we do spend.

—America and the World War[22]

If the father brings up [his children] in such fashion that [they] cannot do anything except spend money . . . he has not helped [them], he has hurt [them].

—*Realizable Ideals* [23]

BRAVERY

Roosevelt made a habit of facing obstacles, then bravely overcoming them.[24] He took up boxing when he was a boy and continued to box throughout his life as an adult. The exercise helped keep him asthma-free. As president, Roosevelt once boxed in a match against a young Navy officer and was punched in the left eye, which permanently blinded that eye. The injury didn't slow him down, though; he continued to read and write as energetically as ever.

The Naval officer who injured Roosevelt never apologized—because the president never told him what happened! "To have told him would have only caused him to feel badly," Roosevelt explained.

Roosevelt continued to display this brand of courage and spirit throughout his presidency, becoming the first chief executive of the White House to ride in a car, an airplane, and a submarine, all extremely dangerous and daring activities at the time!

There are two kinds of courage — moral and
physical — and it is absolutely essential for a [Scout]
to have both if [he or she wishes] to keep [his or her]
own self-respect and to deserve the respect of others.

— "The Essence of Heroism,"
Youth's Companion, April 18, 1901

Every feat of heroism makes us forever
indebted to the [person] who performed it.

— Address, Newport, Rhode Island, June 2, 1897

Bullies do not make brave [people].

— "The American Boy," *St. Nicholas*, May 1900.

It should be [all Scouts'] pride to be
the champions of the weak.

— Address, Washington, D.C., May 24, 1907

CLEANLINESS

It's never easy living up to high expectations, but Theodore Roosevelt Sr. had big plans for his son, and young Theodore worked hard not to let him down.[25] He drank very little alcohol and never smoked, and he never used foul language or repeated off-color or improper jokes.

Throughout his years at Harvard College, he continued faithfully to teach Sunday school.

Ultimately, his father's expectations for him helped Roosevelt establish his own high expectations for himself, and he lived them at all times, especially when leading his own children by his example.

Roosevelt often expressed his expectation of cleanliness in thought, word, and deed:

[Scouts] must be clean-minded and clean-lived, and be able to hold [their] own under all circumstances.

—"The American Boy," *St. Nicholas*, May 1900

To make a good citizen, the prime need is to be decent in thought, clean in mind [and] clean in action.

—Address, Groton, Massachusetts, May 24, 1904

Clean-living, courage [and] self-respect—these qualities are more important in the make-up of a people than [anything else].

—"Mr. Roosevelt's Address," *Outlook*, April 23, 1910

[Citizens] must be clean of life, so that [they] can laugh when [their] public or . . . private record is searched.

—*An Autobiography* [26]

REVERENCE

Throughout his life, Roosevelt loved sports, especially boxing and hunting.[27] Besides being an athlete, he was an enthusiastic spectator and loved nothing more than to attend a rousing sporting event.

Once, when he was in California, Roosevelt was invited to watch a traditional bullfight, which was arranged to showcase the talents of the local Mexican *matadors*, or bullfighters. Roosevelt's hosts were eager to offer him this dramatic spectacle.

Roosevelt thought long and hard before responding. "There are two reasons why I cannot go," he finally said. "One is that I do not like to see a man pitted against a bull, and second, the controlling reason, is that I have an engagement at church at three o'clock."

Though Roosevelt never imposed his religion on others, it heavily influenced his decisions, even when it was tempting to let his church attendance slide a bit.

Roosevelt's belief in the importance of reverence was exhibited by his words:

We must all strive to keep as our most precious heritage the liberty to worship [one's] God as to [one] seems best.

— "The Search for Truth in a Reverent Spirit,"
Outlook, December 2, 1911

The creed, which each [person] in [his or her] heart believes to be essential . . . is for [that person] alone to determine.

— "Civic Helpfulness," *Century Magazine*, October 1900

No democracy can afford to overlook the
vital importance of the ethical and spiritual,
the truly religious elements in life.

— *Through the Brazilian Wilderness*[28]

People who possess either religious belief or
aspiration . . . are going to demand conduct as
the ultimate test of the worth of the belief.

— Address, Berkeley, California, March 26, 1911

CHAPTER THREE

Being Prepared

Roosevelt, using distinctive hand gestures to make his point, speaks in Asheville, North Carolina in September 1902.

Being Prepared

The Scout motto, "Be Prepared," has a very interesting history.[1] From 1901 to 1903, Robert Baden-Powell was in charge of a British military police force set up during the second Boer War at the beginning of the twentieth century. As the story goes, Baden-Powell's men wanted to create a motto that reflected their leader, so they came up with "Be Prepared," incorporating Baden-Powell's initials—B.P.

The famous poet Edwin Markham wrote a poem called "Preparedness," which he sent to Roosevelt:

> *For all your days prepare,*
> *And meet them ever alike:*
> *When you are the anvil, bear it—*
> *When you are the hammer, strike.*

This was one of Roosevelt's favorite poems because it clearly reflected his innermost thinking on the subject. "I shall not only live by these lines myself," wrote Roosevelt to Markham, "but I will also teach my boys to live by them."

Being prepared means thinking ahead. When you're going hiking and you tuck a poncho into your pack because there are dark clouds on the horizon; or having water, batteries, and fuel on hand during hurricane season; or knowing where it's safest and what to do when a tornado hits. Being prepared means being able to coolly and calmly take action in a crisis.

Roosevelt considered being prepared a sacred national duty and believed every American should be ready to defend freedom. He demanded that all Americans be "far-sighted and resolute" when preparing for any job or task. He praised those who worked diligently to prepare for things unforeseen. For Roosevelt, such people were the finest American citizen-leaders of all.

In his personal life, Roosevelt was always prepared. On September 6, 1901, while attending the Pan-American Exposition in Buffalo, New York, President William McKinley was mortally wounded. Vice President Roosevelt was at a luncheon in Lake Champlain, Vermont, when he learned of the tragedy. He calmly advised the news media that the report "appeared to be authentic."

Eight days later, Roosevelt, on a camping trip with his family, received a telegram informing him that President McKinley had died. Understanding that his life had now dramatically changed, he told a close friend that it was unlikely that he would ever see his youthful days again. Roosevelt, whose public service had been preparing him for this moment all of his adult life, became the twenty-sixth president of the United States.

LET [A SCOUT] BE UNSELFISH AND GENTLE AS WELL AS STRONG AND BRAVE.

"It is a dreadful thing to come into the presidency in this way," he said on his first day as the country's top executive. "Here is the task, and I have got to do it to the best of my ability." He would serve almost two full terms and be forever remembered as one of our greatest presidents.

He frequently spoke and wrote on the topic of always being prepared:

Do what you can, with what you have, where you are.
—Through the Brazilian Wilderness [2]

Half-preparation is no preparation at all.
—The Foes of Our Own Household [3]

Preparedness must be of the soul,
no less than of the body.
—Letter to S. Stanwood Menken, January 10, 1917

Unless we prepare in advance we cannot,
when the crisis comes, be true to ourselves.
—Address, Chicago, Illinois, April 29, 1916

To prepare a little, but not much, stands on par with
a city developing a fire department which, after a
fire occurs, can put it out a little, but not much.
—Address, Detroit, Michigan, May 19, 1916

CHAPTER FOUR

A Good Turn

Roosevelt extending his hand from a reviewing platform at Cheyenne, Wyoming, in April 1911.

A Good Turn

Robert Baden-Powell first wrote about the "Good Turn" around 1901 when answering letters from boys who admired his military heroism.[1]

The Boy Scouts of America, who adopted as their slogan, "Do a Good Turn Daily," due to the good deed done by an unknown English Boy Scout to William D. Boyce, a Chicago businessman lost in London in 1909. As the story goes, the young man led Mr. Boyce to his destination and later to Scout Headquarters. He acquired Scouting literature to bring back to the United States, and Boyce incorporated the Boy Scouts of America in Washington, D.C., on February 8, 1910, soon after his return.

An enduring image in the lore of the Boy Scouts of America is of the young Scout who helps an elderly woman across the street. Scouts have dedicated millions of hours of service by doing good turns to others. During World War I, the Boy Scouts of America mobilized countless Scouts to support American soldiers overseas by planting victory gardens to lessen the strain on domestic food supplies, collecting metal scrap by the ton, selling war bonds, counting the supply of black walnut trees used for airplane propeller blades and

EVERY [SCOUT] OUGHT TO TRAIN THEMSELVES TO DO [THEIR] FULL DUTY TO THE COMMUNITY.

gun stocks, and many other projects to support the war effort.

"You insist on the doing of a good turn daily to somebody without reward," Roosevelt wrote Executive Secretary James E. West in 1911, "and thus furnish the elements of a national, widespread American courtesy."

In 1906, Roosevelt won the Nobel Prize for helping bring about the peace treaty that ended the war between Russia and Japan. In addition to the medal, he received a large cash prize equal to about $800,000 today. Though tempted to keep the prize for himself, Roosevelt determined that it really belonged to the American people. "I hated to come to that decision," he wrote his son Kermit, "because I very much wished the extra money to leave to all you children."

By late 1918, the money had been disbursed to twenty-eight charities throughout the country in support of U.S. relief services during World War I.

Roosevelt believed in doing good deeds, and he commented about this in many of his writings:

The doer is better than the critic.

—*American Ideals and Other Essays* [2]

Work with your whole heart in all things.

— "The American Boy," *St. Nicholas*, May 1900

*Let each [Scout] try to render service to others,
and try to do well in every task that comes
to [his or her] hands, big or little.*

—Letter to James E. West, February 10, 1911

*Service is the true test by which a [person's]
worth should be judged.*

—"Where We Cannot Work with Socialists,"
Outlook, March 20, 1909

*Every good citizen, whatever [their] condition, owes
[their] first service to those who are nearest to [them].*

—Address, Chicago, Illinois, September 3, 1900

Money can never take the place of service.

—"Reform through Social Work," *McClure's*, March 1901

Success comes only to those who lead the life of endeavor.

—*Strenuous Epigrams of Theodore Roosevelt*[3]

*[Scouts] who [do their] best work, [do] it because
[they are] drawn to it by an irresistible power.*

—*Theodore Roosevelt: His Life and Work*[4]

CHAPTER FIVE

The Outdoor Code

Roosevelt at Glacier Point in Yosemite National Park in May 1903.

The Outdoor Code

*T*he Outdoor Code first appeared in the fifth edition of the Boy Scouts of America's *Handbook for Boys* in 1948.[1] World War II was over, and millions of soldiers were home and beginning to populate undeveloped land and consume the natural resources of our country at a great rate. One consequence was a sudden boom in home building as young veterans started families. The Outdoor Code was placed in the "Do Your Part" section of the *Handbook* because every Scout was to take personal responsibility in preserving the nation's national resources as best they could:

> *As an American, I will do my best to*
> *Be clean in my outdoor manners,*
> *Be careful with fire,*
> *Be considerate in the outdoors,*
> *and be conservation-minded.*

Respect for nature is another important element in the makeup of a good citizen-leader. Even as a ten-year-old boy, Roosevelt had a conscious concern for the environment, writing that he "mourned the cutting down of a tree." As one of the most conservation-minded presidents, Roosevelt the conservationist was a forceful proponent of the national duty to protect the environment. As president, he set aside more land for national parks and nature preserves than the first twenty-five presidents combined. By the end of his presidency, he had protected 230 million acres, including millions of acres of national forests and wildlife refuges and national treasures like the Grand Canyon in Arizona and Mesa Verde National Park in Colorado.

Roosevelt started studying natural history as a boy of seven and pursued this interest for the rest of his life.

LET IT BE A POINT OF HONOR TO PROTECT BIRDS, TREES, AND FLOWERS.

When still a young boy, Roosevelt was walking up Broadway in New York City when he came upon a vendor displaying a dead seal from the nearby harbor. Fascinated, he took out a folding pocket rule and took all sorts of measurements that he dutifully scribbled into his notebook. Eventually, he was given the seal's skull, which he used to start his own personal collection of nature artifacts that he assembled in the "Roosevelt Museum of Natural History" in his home, emulating his father, a founder of the American Museum of Natural History on Central Park West in New York City.

Today, when climate change, endangered species, and other dangers to the environment are so much in the news, Roosevelt was a century ahead of his time:

Conservation is a great moral issue for it involves the patriotic duty of ensuring the safety and continuance of the nation.

—Address, "The New Nationalism,"
Osawatomie, Kansas, August 31, 1910

The conservation of natural resources is the fundamental problem. Unless we solve that problem, it will avail us little to solve all others.

—Address, Memphis, Tennessee, October 4, 1907

When you help to preserve our forests or to plant new ones, you are acting the part of good citizens.

—Address, "Arbor Day Message to School Children," Washington, D.C., April 15, 1907

We are fast learning that trees must not be cut down more rapidly than they are being replaced.

—"The Conservation of Wild Life," *Outlook*, January 20, 1915

The movement for the conservation of wildlife and the larger movement for the conservation of all our natural resources are essentially democratic in spirit, purpose, and method.

—*A Book-Lover's Holidays in the Open* [2]

It is an incalculable added pleasure to anyone's sum of happiness if he or she grows to know . . . the wonder-book of nature.

—*Outdoor Pastimes of an American Hunter* [3]

CHAPTER SIX

Character
Counts

A formal portrait of Roosevelt taken as a private citizen around 1910.

Character Counts

Roosevelt considered character the "foundation stone of national life" and saw it as a critical element in the making of a citizen-leader.[1] He understood that the Scout Oath, Law, motto, slogan, and Outdoor Code all worked together to build good character.

In a landmark speech delivered in 1910 in Osawatomie, Kansas, Roosevelt said that "the most important elements in any man's career must be the sum of those qualities which, in the aggregate, we speak of as character." He expected his associates to exhibit a high degree of personal morality. That is one of the reasons he admired Scouting so much. But to demand such a high code of conduct, he had to set an outstanding example and practice what he preached. He did so as a young man and continued to do so all his life.

While studying at Harvard in February 1878, Roosevelt was devastated by the death of his father.

POLITENESS AND GOOD MANNERS MUST NOT BE NEGLECTED.

When he returned to school after the funeral, he realized that along with bearing his grief for the loss of his beloved father, he would also have to carry the financial burden of paying for the rest of his education with his inheritance. He refocused on his studies and two weeks later was able to score near perfect marks on his exams. He continued to regularly teach

Sunday school class while in college and to exercise daily, remaining ever mindful of his father's sage advice: "Take care of your morals first, your health next, and finally your studies."

Roosevelt spent the rest of his life teaching his children his own father's lessons about values and morals. He also shared those values with millions of children across the nation through speeches, articles, and personal letters.

The following quotations are just a few of the many words that Roosevelt spoke on the importance of character:

It is character that counts in a nation as in a [Scout].

—Address, Galena, Illinois, April 27, 1900

The [Scout] who is going to make a great [citizen-leader] . . . must make up [his or her] mind not merely to overcome a thousand obstacles but to win in spite of a thousand repulses or defeats.

—"Character and Success," *Outlook*, March 31, 1900

It is hard to fail, but it is worse never to have tried to succeed.

—*The Strenuous Life* [2]

Though intellect stands high, character stands higher.

—Address, Oxford, England, June 7, 1910

*Perhaps there is no more important
component of character than steadfast resolution.*

—"Character and Success," *Outlook*, March 31, 1900

*I do the things that I believe ought to be done.
And when I make up my mind to do a thing, I act.*

—*Theodore Roosevelt on Leadership*[3]

*It is not what [Scouts work] at . . .
it is the way [they] work at it.*

—*Strenuous Epigrams of Theodore Roosevelt*[4]

*The welfare of each of us is dependent
fundamently upon the welfare of all of us.*

—Address, "A Square Deal," Syracuse,
New York, September 7, 1903

*Success—the real success—does not depend upon
the position you hold, but upon how you
carry yourself in that position.*

—Address, Cambridge, England, May 26, 1910

*Far and away the best prize that life offers is
the chance to work hard at work worth doing.*

—Address, "A Square Deal," Syracuse,
New York, September 7, 1903

CHAPTER SEVEN

Being a
Citizen-Leader

Roosevelt speaking at New Castle, Wyoming, in May 1903.

Being a Citizen-Leader

R*oosevelt and the Boy Scouts of America* shared the common goal of creating a better American citizen-leader.[1] "My aim is to make the . . . citizen . . . feel that [he or she] must have a pride in [his or her] American citizenship," Roosevelt declared in 1907. He believed that only when Americans took pride in their citizenship could the country lead the world by moral example, allowing the United States to exert a positive influence on global politics. In Roosevelt's vision of America, citizens would be judged by their deeds alone. "We are Americans," he told an audience in Lincoln, Nebraska. "We can do nothing . . . unless we feel with all our hearts, devotion to this country."

Roosevelt set an example for all of us to follow. He believed that it was his duty, and that of his family, to serve the nation with dedication, whether this meant running for office or volunteering for military duty. Both had allowed him to strongly influence the direction of the country through his inspirational style of leadership.

By the age of twenty-three, Roosevelt was a member of the New York State Assembly where he made himself a "perfect nuisance" with proposed laws intended to limit the profits of industrial tycoons who robbed the pocketbooks of the common citizen. The *New York Times* declared: "Every good citizen has cause for rejoicing."

When he was thirty, President Benjamin Harrison appointed him as one of New York City's three civil service commissioners. Roosevelt sought to rid the city's government of all wrongdoers and eliminate many corrupt policies, like only hiring friends of high-ranking officials. In the end, he successfully cleaned up the government because he refused to compromise on what he knew was right.

Eight years later, he became one of New York City's four police commissioners in charge of the four sections of the city. Immediately, Roosevelt was elected the president of their board due to his reputation for moral and honest action. He was so effective at reducing crime in the city that he earned another appointment, this time as the undersecretary of the Navy. He then became one of the most famous men in America by leading his Rough Riders during the Spanish-American War. Returning a hero, he was elected the governor of New York at the age of forty.

In November 1900, Roosevelt assumed the duties of vice president of the United States. At the age of forty-two, he ascended to the presidency when President McKinley was assassinated, remaining today the youngest man ever to assume the office of U.S. president (though John F. Kennedy, at forty-three, won the distinction of being the youngest president voted into office).

MIND, EYE [AND] MUSCLE MUST BE TRAINED SO THAT [A SCOUT] CAN MASTER [HIMSELF OR HERSELF].

Roosevelt devoted his life to serving his fellow citizens and lent his name to those organizations that best represented all that was good for the country. One of his favorites was the Boy Scouts of America.

By the time Roosevelt died in January 1919, the positive image of the Boy Scouts of America was impressed on the American consciousness. The Boy Scouts of America of today can thank its first and only Chief Scout Citizen, Theodore Roosevelt, for giving it a strong foundation on which to establish its celebrated program of building citizen-leaders.

In Roosevelt's words:

In American citizenship, we can succeed permanently only upon the basis of standing shoulder to shoulder . . . each working for all.

—Address, Chattanooga, Tennessee, September 8, 1902

Intelligence and courage are as necessary as honesty is to good citizenship.

—"The Essence of Heroism," *Youth's Companion*, April 18, 1901

It is a necessary thing to have good laws, good institutions, but the most necessary of all things is to have a high quality of individual citizenship.

—Address, Provincetown, Massachusetts, August 20, 1907

Courage is a prime necessity for [a] citizen if [he or she] is to be a good citizen.

—Address, Cambridge, Massachusetts, February 23, 1907

*Good citizenship consists in doing the many
small duties, private and public, which in
the aggregate make it up.*

—Address, Arlington, Virginia, May 21, 1902

*People ask the difference between a leader
and a boss . . . the leader leads and the boss drives.*

—Address, Binghamton, New York, October 24, 1910

Example is the most potent of all things.

—Theodore Roosevelt on Leadership [2]

*Courage, honesty, and common sense are
essential to good citizenship; joined with
courtesy and consideration for others.*

— Written sentiment, Spokane, Washington, April 8, 1911

*The good citizen must be a good citizen in
[his or her] own country first before [he or she]
can . . . be a citizen of the world.*

—Theodore Roosevelt Cyclopedia [3]

CHAPTER EIGHT

Final Thoughts

Roosevelt greets the crowd gathered outside Union Station in Washington, D.C during his presidency.

8

Final Thoughts

*I wonder if he knows it—how the boys
     are thinking of him,
The sturdy little youngsters who all idolize
     and love him!
The kids that wear Rough-Rider suits or
     play with Teddy bears,
Who charge a hill at sleepy-time when they
     Climb up the stairs—
I wonder if he knows it—why, the sorrow
     Of their feeling
Is full of all the balm there is and wonderful
     With healing.*

*I wonder if he knows it—how the children
     Ask for "Teddy,"
For children's hearts to show their faith
     Are ever firm and ready.
From golden California to the rocky coast
     of Maine
The hearts of all the youngsters throb to
     Sympathy's refrain.
I wonder if he knows it—how the boys are
     thinking of him!
Unselfish, loyal little chaps—a world of good
     'twould do him.*

—Wilbur D. Nesbit

75

Theodore Roosevelt's words hold as much value for Americans today as when he spoke them or wrote them down.[1] His vision of shaping the country's citizens into leaders and role models for the community, nation, and world is as essential today as it was then.

Roosevelt communicated with young people through caring words, thoughts, and deeds. And they responded! Often when on holiday from the White House at Sagamore Hill, his home on Long Island, Roosevelt organized long horseback rides for local children along with his own.

EACH [SCOUT] SHOULD MAKE UP [HIS OR HER] MIND THAT [HE OR SHE] WILL DO [THEIR] PART IN SERVING THE NATION AS A WHOLE.

During one such outing, a big thunderstorm blew in, but the children remained happy and upbeat. One little boy later confessed to being frightened, but said that "confidence in Colonel Roosevelt gave [him] courage to meet the storm." On another trip, Roosevelt took an unexpected tumble into the water. "There goes our daddy," yelled one of the local lads. Seemingly, every child that Roosevelt came into contact with felt the same way—he was "daddy."

When Theodore Roosevelt passed away in the early hours of January 6, 1919, the nation mourned. Franklin K. Lane, Interior Secretary to President Woodrow Wilson, eloquently summed up Roosevelt's fast-emerging legacy:

> We may surely expect to see developed a Roosevelt legend, a body of tales that will exalt the physical power and endurance of the man and the boldness of his spirit, his robust capacity for blunt speech and his hearty comradeship, his

live interest in all things living—these will make
our boys for the long future proud that they are
of his . . . country. And no surer fame than this
can come to any man—to live in the hearts of the
boys of his land as one whose doings and sayings
they would wish to make their own.

Within months after his passing, testimonial and
remembrance books appeared in bookstores across the
country. Roosevelt was lauded as the "great heart" and
the "American prophet." The Boy Scouts of America was
especially saddened. In a letter to Edith Roosevelt, his
widow, Chief Scout Executive West noted Roosevelt's
special significance to Scouts. "In losing Colonel
Roosevelt," West wrote, "our boys and indeed the whole
world have sustained a great loss." West pledged to keep
Roosevelt's memory alive to "stimulate the boyhood of
our country . . . to better citizenship" through service,
informing her that the organization's Executive Board
that morning had asked every Scout unit to plant "one or
more sturdy trees" in his memory.

Planting trees had become a ritual through which
Americans honored their countrymen who had given
their lives in World War I. *American Forestry* magazine
in 1919 called such trees "a new form of monument—
the memorial that lives." So it seemed appropriate to
perform such service in honor of the country's leading
voice for conservation.

Within days, Scout troops nationwide announced
their intention to plant memorial trees. Some sought
to plant enough to form Roosevelt memorial groves
and one group planted 500 seedlings that together
formed the letters "TR." The most prized seeds came

from a large black walnut tree shading his grave that provided many bushels of nuts. But within a few years, this tree could not keep up with the massive demand for its walnuts. In memoriam, National Scout Commissioner Dan Beard had hundreds of nuts collected to "scatter all over the country" in the hands of Scout executives.

At the dedication of the Roosevelt Memorial Tree in Audubon Park in New Orleans, Louisiana, Governor John M. Parker recalled an event years before when he invited Roosevelt to visit and the great man entertained neighborhood children. In the library at Parker's home, Roosevelt, with his sleeves rolled up, at ease on a great wicker chair, regaled the children with an account of his lion hunt in Africa. At the Audubon Park ceremony, two Scouts approached Parker and saluted. "We will eternally keep watch on that tree," they said, "because we were two of the boys who listened to his splendid story of the lion hunt, which we will never forget as long as we live."

> I BELIEVE HEARTILY IN THE WORK YOUR ASSOCIATION IS DOING.

In September 1919, members of the newly formed Roosevelt Memorial Association marched from Buffalo, New York, to his grave at Oyster Bay, Long Island, starting off with an American flag of silk with no stars in the blue union patch. Scouts and high school students escorted the flag most of the way. At each stop, a white star was hand-sewn onto the flag. The forty-eighth and final star was added at Roosevelt's gravesite in Youngs Cemetery when the memorial flag arrived in Oyster Bay on October 27, that would have been Roosevelt's sixty-first birthday. Dignitaries from around the world attended the ceremony, including King Albert and Queen Elizabeth of Belgium.

Beard, deeply moved, led a small contingent of Scouts to Roosevelt's grave a year later in November. West decided to make this show of respect an annual event and called it the "Roosevelt Pilgrimage." From a small gathering of Scouts in the first year in 1920, attendance rose to more than 6,000 a decade later. Over the next thirty years, a special Scout memorial program included patriotic songs, recitations, and speeches that the *New York Times* diligently reported into the early 1950s:

The New York Times
October 29, 1921

OYSTER BAY, L.I.—Eulogizing the late Colonel Theodore Roosevelt as an American and a true Scout, more than a thousand members of the Boy Scouts of America paid tribute at his grave this afternoon at Youngs Memorial Cemetery. They presented an impressive scene kneeling in silent prayer at the close of the exercises.

The Scouts, who came from all parts of Long Island, New Jersey, Brooklyn and Manhattan, under the leadership of Colonel Daniel Beard, National Scout Commissioner and an old friend of the late president, made their second annual pilgrimage to the grave.

Headed by a band, the boys marched to the cemetery with members of the Camp Fire Club of America. Hundreds of spectators followed the boys, all uncovering as the band played "The Star-Spangled Banner."

At the grave Colonel Beard then made a short address telling of the late president's Americanism and his pleasure at being made honorary president of the Scout organization. Colonel Beard urged the boys to follow the life of the Colonel and lead good clean lives. Dr. [Charles A.] Eastman declared that Colonel Roosevelt was a "red-blooded American" whose memory would live forever.

Following taps, fifty boys, one by one passed the grave, dropping wreaths. The Oath of the Scouts was then repeated, and at its conclusion Colonel Beard, kneeling, placed the wreath on the grave while the Scouts and hundreds of spectators knelt in a brief silent prayer.

As a touching tribute, the local council in Nassau County, now known as the Theodore Roosevelt Council, has a special way of honoring this great man and great American. Since 1973, they have presented the "Chief Scout Citizen Award" to a special supporter in their community, one who has made a positive impact for better Scouting. The Scouts themselves have another way. These days when they gather around the campfire at Camp Wauwepex at the Schiff Scout Reservation in Wading River, New York, there is always an empty seat in the council ring, forever reserved for Theodore Roosevelt, once and always Chief Scout Citizen of the Boy Scouts of America.

National Scout Commissioner Dan Beard lays a memorial wreath at Roosevelt's grave in
Oyster Bay, Long Island, during the tenth Roosevelt Pilgrimage in October 1929.

Appendix A

The Boy Scouts of America's Resolution
on Theodore Roosevelt
by Hermann Hagedorn

He was found faithful over a few things and he was made ruler over many; he cut his own trail clean and straight and millions followed him toward the light.[1]

He was frail; he made himself a tower of strength. He was timid; he made himself a lion of courage. He was a dreamer; he became one of the great doers of all time.

Men put their trust in him; women found a champion in him; kings stood in awe of him, but children made him their playmate.

He broke a nation's slumber with his cry, and it rose up. He touched the eyes of blind men with a flame and gave them vision. Souls became swords through him; swords became servants of God.

He was loyal to his country, and he exacted loyalty; he loved many lands, but he loved his own land best.

He was terrible in battle, but tender to the weak; joyous and tireless, being free from self-pity; clean with a cleanness that cleansed the air like a gale.

His courtesy knew no wealth or class; his friendship, no creed or color or race. His courage stood every

Roosevelt reviewing a Scout troop at Sagamore Hill on Long Island in 1916.

onslaught of savage beast and ruthless man, of loneliness, of victory, of defeat. His mind was eager, his heart was true, his body and spirit defiant of obstacles, ready to meet what might come.

He fought injustice and tyranny; bore sorrow gallantly; loved all nature, bleak spaces and hardy companions, hazardous adventure and the zest of battle. Wherever he went he carried his own pack; and in the uttermost parts of the earth he kept his conscience for his guide.

Appendix B

"The American Boy" and Selected Letters
to the Boy Scouts of America

Of *course what we have a right* to expect of the American boy is that he shall turn out to be a good American man.[1] The boy can best become a good man by being a good boy—not a goody-goody boy, but just a plain good boy.

I do not mean that he must love only the negative virtues; I mean that he must love the positive virtues also. "Good," in the largest sense, should include whatever is fine, straightforward, clean, and manly. The best boys I know—the best men I know—are good at their studies or their business, fearless and stalwart, hated and feared by all that is wicked and depraved; incapable of submitting to wrongdoing, and equally incapable of being aught but tender to the weak and helpless.

Of course the effect that a thoroughly manly, thoroughly straight and upright boy can have upon the companions of his own age, and upon those who are younger, is incalculable. If he is not thoroughly manly, then they will not respect him, and his good qualities will count for but little; while of course, if he is mean, cruel or wicked, then his physical strength

Roosevelt with Troop 4 of Garden City, New York, in May 1916.

and force of mind merely make him so much the more objectionable a member of society.

He can not do good work if he is not strong and does not try with his whole heart and soul to count in any contest; and his strength will be a curse to himself and to every one else if he does not have a thorough command over himself and over his own evil passions, and if he does not use his strength on the side of decency, justice, and fair dealing.

In short, in life, as in a football game,
the principle to follow is: Hit the line hard;
don't foul and don't shirk, but hit the line hard.

SELECTED LETTERS TO THE BOY SCOUTS OF AMERICA

September 23, 1910

Dear Mr. [Chief Scout] Ernest Thompson Seton:

The excessive development of city life in modern industrial civilization, which has seen its climax here in our own country, is accompanied by a very unhealthy atrophying of some of the essential virtues which must be embodied in any [person] who is to be a . . . really good citizen.

Your movement aims at counteracting these unhealthy tendencies. I heartily wish all success to the movement.

Sincerely yours,
Theodore Roosevelt

February 10, 1911

Mr. [Executive Secretary] James E. West
My dear Sir:

I earnestly believe in the Boy Scout movement because I see the national possibility of this movement among boys. There are several things which we should see in the lives of our American boys. They should grow up strong and alert, able to stand the strain of an honest day's hard work, and of an honest attempt to help forward the material and moral progress of our nation.

American boyhood should be resourceful and inventive so that the American man of the future may be ever ready to help in the hour of the nation's need. American boys should always show good manners, and the desire to help all who are in trouble or difficulty and indeed to help the weak at all times. Courtesy is as much the mark of a gentleman as truthfulness and courage, and every American boy should be a gentleman, fearless in defending his own rights and the rights of the weak, and scrupulous to inflict no wrong on others. The boy who is to grow into the right kind of man should scorn lying as he scorns cowardice, and he should remember that [one] is always considerate of and courteous towards others. In this nation of ours, the ideal of everyone should be to help in the work of all. Therefore let each boy try to render service to others, and try to do well in every task that comes to his hands, big or little. The boys of America should understand our institutions and their history; they should know of the lives of the great men that have blazed the trail for our national greatness, and of the mighty deeds that they wrought; they should feel a high pride of country and a real spirit of patriotism, which will make them emulate these careers of gallant and efficient service and of willingness to make sacrifices for the sake of a lofty ideal. American boys should grow up understanding the life of the community about them, and appreciating the privileges and the duties of citizenship, so that they may face the great questions of national life with the ability and resolute purpose to help in solving them aright. Each boy should make up his mind that . . . he will do his part in serving the nation as a whole.

I believe heartily in the work your Association is doing. . . . You insist on the doing of a good turn daily to somebody without reward, and thus furnish the elements of a national, widespread American courtesy. You try to teach boys to do things for themselves and so make them resourceful. You stand for true patriotism, true citizenship, true Americanism. I wish all success to a movement fraught with such good purposes.

Faithfully Yours,
Theodore Roosevelt

July 20, 1911

Mr. [Executive Secretary] James E. West
My dear Sir,

The Boy Scout movement is of peculiar importance to the whole country. It has already done much good, and it will do far more, for it is in its essence a practical scheme through which to impart a proper standard of ethical conduct, proper standards of fair play and consideration for others, and courage and decency, to boys who have never been reached and never will be reached by the ordinary type of preaching, lay or clerical.

The movement is one for efficiency and patriotism. It does not try to make soldiers of Boy Scouts, but to make boys who will turn out as men to be fine citizens, and who will, if their country needs them, make better soldiers for having been Scouts. No one can be a good American unless he is a good citizen, and every boy ought to train himself so that as a man he will be able to do his full duty to the community. I want to see the Boy Scouts not merely utter fine sentiments, but act on them; not merely sing, "My Country 'Tis of Thee," but act in a way that will give them a country to be proud of. . . . I hope the Boy Scouts will practice truth and square dealing, and courage and honesty, so that when as young men they begin to take a part not only in earning their own livelihood, but in governing the community, they may be able to show in practical fashion their insistence upon the great truth . . . directly related to every-day life. Indeed the boys even while only boys can have a very real effect upon the conduct of the grown up members of the community, for decency and square dealing are just as contagious as vice and corruption.

Every healthy boy ought to feel . . . it is necessary to have a constructive, and not merely a destructive, nature; and if he can keep this feeling as he grows up he has taken his first step toward good citizenship. The boy can do an immense amount right in the present, entirely aside from training himself to be a good citizen in the future; and he can only do this if he associates himself with other boys. Let the Boy Scouts see to it that the best use is made of the parks and playgrounds in their villages and home towns. A gang of toughs may make a playground impossible; and if the Boy Scouts in the neighborhood of that particular playground are fit for their work, they will show that they won't permit any such gang of toughs to have its way. Moreover, let the Boy Scouts take the lead in seeing that the parks and playgrounds are turned to a really good account. I hope, by the way, that one of the prime teachings among the Boy Scouts will be the teaching against vandalism. Let it be a point of honor to protect birds, trees and flowers, and so to make our country more beautiful and not more ugly because we have lived in it.

The Boy Scouts must war against the same foes and vices that most hurt the nation; and they must try to develop the same virtues that the nation most needs. . . . Let the boy stand stoutly against his enemies both from without and from within, let him show courage in confronting fearlessly one set of enemies, and in controlling and mastering the others. [Every] boy [must have] courage, courage to stand up against the forces of evil, and courage to stand up in the right path. Let him be unselfish and gentle, as well as strong and brave. It should be a matter of pride to him that he is not afraid of anyone, and that he scorns not to be gentle and considerate to everyone, and especially to those who are weaker than he is. . . . Don't ever forget to let the boy know that courtesy, politeness, and good manners must not be neglected. They are not little things, because they are used at every turn in daily life. Let the boy remember also that in addition to courage, unselfishness, and fair dealing, he must have efficiency, he must have knowledge, he must cultivate a sound body and a good mind, and train himself so that he can act with quick decision in any crisis that may arise. Mind, eye, muscle, all must be trained so that the boy can master himself, and thereby learn to master his fate. I heartily wish all good luck to the movement.

Very Sincerely Yours,
Theodore Roosevelt

December 10, 1915

Mr. [Chief Scout Executive] James E. West
My dear Mr. West:

The Boy Scouts like all the other boys of the country should get into their heads clearly the idea that a true democracy involves . . . obligations and service in time of need and that a [leader] who admits [their] obligations and makes no adequate preparation to discharge it is a poor citizen.

The Boy Scouts should be sedulously trained so that they can act together, and at the same time each increase his individual self-reliance. There must always be the power of acting in cooperation with others and the willingness and ability to accept responsibility and to act on one's own individual initiative. The virtues of courtesy, kindliness, unselfishness, desire to help others, and desire to join with others for mutual help must all be encouraged. Together with these virtues, we must also encourage the sterner virtues which milder ones amount to so little.

As the Boy Scout develops in body and soul he must learn not only to treat others well, but to be able to interfere to prevent injustices by the strong against the weak. These two sets of qualities are indispensable in private life and they are no less indispensable in national and international life.

The Boy Scout movement is distinctively an asset to our country for the development of efficiency . . . and good citizenship. It is essential that its leaders be . . . of strong, wholesome character, of unmistakable devotion to our country, its customs and ideals as well as in soul and by law citizens thereof, whose whole-hearted loyalty is given to this nation and to this nation alone.

With all good wishes,
Sincerely Yours,
Theodore Roosevelt

Appendix C

"Address to the 1929 Theodore Roosevelt Pilgrimage"
by National Scout Commissioner Dan Beard

We are here today for the tenth time to pledge our allegiance to the patriotism, independence, and . . . courage of the distinguished outdoor man, our great Chief Scout Citizen, Theodore Roosevelt.[1]

The fraternity of the great outdoors bids or pledges a man to join its ranks. It does not send a delegate to tap the candidate on the back or speak to him orally. Its appeal is of a spiritual nature and is communicated to the soul of the man, and every man, woman or child who receives that call must respond, for it is not only an invitation, but, a demand, an order from the Great Mystery, the Commander-in-Chief, which must be obeyed.

Over three hundred years ago a small, shivering group of people who feared nothing but Almighty God, landed upon the bleak and forbidding shores of New England, searching for a place where they would be free from religious persecution. These people had their faults, but dishonesty and cowardice were not among them, nor did they lack high ideals. They were a band of dreamers, and as I have often times remarked, be it known, that this old world of ours does but mark time between the advent of dreamers.

Scouts bearing American flags lead the procession of 4,000 pilgrims
to Roosevelt's grave during the tenth Roosevelt Pilgrimage in October
1929 at Oyster Bay, Long Island.

Over a century later, another band of dreamers,
including [Alexander] Hamilton, [Thomas] Jefferson,
[Benjamin] Franklin and [George] Washington did not
hesitate to risk their heads in order that the fulfillment of
their dreams might be realized.

America today is a realization of the dreams of those
early adventurers. America today is a product of envi-
ronments and education, which is but another name
for development. It is but one of the stages of social
evolution. The Declaration of Independence was directly evolved from the Magna Carta, and the whole idea of
Democracy, as we now understand it, is but the evolution
of the religious convictions of man. We believe that we are
born to be of use to our fellow men and must, by example
and precept, strive to make this a better world in which

to live. Boy Scouts and Scoutmasters particularly appreciate the fact that the success of the United States of America today is a result of the strenuous . . . lives led by such men as President Roosevelt, the early Americans and the buckskin clan men of our railroads, the men whose campfires marked the sites of our great cities.

Happiness is largely dependent upon a normal life; but normal life does not exist always in the palace, the hovel or crowded tenements. Where then may we find it? It flourishes best in the open; but yon walnut tree, massive, [and] strong . . . is but an educated walnut tree whose vitality might have been killed or crippled by a tiny worm or that might have withered and dried for lack of proper earth and water.

We are optimists; we have great faith in humanity. Pessimism and gloom are abnormal conditions and find no place with us. We know that there are few normal experiences in life that do not possess a bright side. But equally true is it that all normal experiences have a serious side, so let us choose to look upon the serious side of outdoor life, deeming it something more than objectless recreation or frivolous occupation. Outdoor pursuits should no longer be classified simply as sports, but recognized as a vitally important part of education.

On top of yon hill rests the mortal remains of . . . a typical outdoor man who loved the clouds above him and the earth beneath his foot, in which his body is now resting. Whenever I met discouragement in my campaign for the boys and the open, it was Theodore Roosevelt's bright smile and shining glasses that cheered me on. The first public speech I ever made in my life was on the platform with Theodore Roosevelt . . . and the most unique compliment I have ever had paid me from the outdoor world was when a band of . . . Apache Indians formed three troops of Scouts; one named after Theodore Roosevelt, one after their great chief, Geronimo, and one after my unworthy self. It is such incidents, combined with a firm conviction that all normal boys are naturally outdoor Scouts that have encouraged me to keep up this fight for fifty-one years. We do not see victory ahead because IT IS HERE! Theodore Roosevelt . . . our Chief Scout Citizen and now our spiritual leader, we believe and feel is with us today, inspiring all these boys and ourselves with renewed devotion to everything which tends to healthy, wholesome manhood, clean lives, and a noble purpose.

While in camp at [the 1929 World Jamboree in England] with between forty and sixty thousand boys encamped around us, [Executive Board member] Mortimer Schiff said to me: "You should be the happiest man alive. You have lived to see all your dreams realized."

One of those dreams is the presence of you boys, you men, and you people here today to honor our Chief Scout Citizen who never missed an opportunity to honor us.

Roosevelt in his library at Sagamore Hill, Long Island, in 1905.

Notes

Introduction

1. Stories that begin the introduction are adapted from Daniel
   Carter Beard, *The Autobiography of Dan Beard,* a draft from
   the Library of Congress; Allen H. Anderson, *The Chief: Ernest
   Thompson Seton and the Changing West* (College Station: Texas
   A&M University Press, 1986); and William H. Kniffin, *Thirty
   Years of Scouting in Nassau* (Massapequa, New York: Theodore
   Roosevelt Council, Boy Scouts of America, 1999); Clara Barrus,
   The Life and Letters of John Burroughs. 2 vols. (Boston: Houghton
   Mifflin, 1925); David Von Drehle, "The Myth About Boys," *Time,*
   July 26, 2007; Donald J. Davidson, ed., *The Wisdom of Theodore
   Roosevelt* (New York: Citadel Press, 2003). Roosevelt's quotations
   come from letters in The National Archives of the Boy Scouts of
   America and from the Raab Collection.

Chapter 1

1. Stories that begin this section are adapted from Edmund
   Morris, *The Rise of Theodore Roosevelt* (New York: Modern
   Library, 2001) and the Theodore Roosevelt Association's web
   site: www.theodoreroosevelt.org (accessed February 2007).
2. Stories that begin this section are adapted from George
   DeWan, "From Long Island to Over There, www.newsday.com
   /community/guide/lihistory/ny-history-hs709a,0,7616454.story
   (accessed July 2007).
3. Theodore Roosevelt, *Oliver Cromwell* (New York: Charles
   Scribner's Sons, 1900).
4. Ibid.
5. Stories that begin this section are adapted from H. W. Brands,
   TR: The Last Romantic (New York: Basic Books, 1997); Carleton B.
   Case, *Good Stories about Roosevelt: The Humorous Side of a Great*

American (Chicago: Shrewesbury, 1920); and Frederick Wood, *Roosevelt as We Knew Him* (Philadelphia: Winston, 1954).

6. Theodore Roosevelt, *American Ideals and Other Essays* (New York: G.P. Putnam's Sons, 1915).

7. Theodore Roosevelt, *Fear God and Take Your Own Part* (New York: George H. Doran, 1916).

8. Hermann Hagedorn, ed., *The Americanism of Theodore Roosevelt: Selections from His Writings and Speeches* (Boston: Houghton Mifflin, 1923).

9. Stories that begin this section are adapted from Brands, *TR: The Last Romantic*.

10. Frederick E. Drinker and Jay Henry Mowbray, eds., *Theodore Roosevelt: His Life and Work* (Washington, D.C.: National, 1919).

11. Roosevelt, *American Ideals and Other Essays.*

12. Theodore Roosevelt, *Strenuous Epigrams of Theodore Roosevelt* (New York: H.M. Caldwell, 1904).

13. Theodore Roosevelt, *The Strenuous Life: Essays and Addresses* (New York: Century, 1901).

14. Stories that begin this section are adapted from Case, *Good Stories about Roosevelt*; Drinker and Mowbray, *Theodore Roosevelt;* and Wood, *Roosevelt as We Knew Him.*

15. Roosevelt, *Strenuous Epigrams of Theodore Roosevelt.*

16. Stories that begin this section are adapted from Theodore Roosevelt, *African Game Trails: An Account of the African Wanderings of an American Hunter-Naturalist* (New York: Charles Scribner's Sons, 1910); Wood, *Roosevelt as We Knew Him;* and www.theodoreroosevelt.org.

17. Roosevelt, *American Ideals and Other Essays.*

18. Stories that begin this section are adapted from Edmund Morris, *Theodore Rex* (New York: Modern Library, 2001).

19. Theodore Roosevelt, *Realizable Ideals* (San Francisco: Whitaker & Ray-Wiggin, 1912).

20. Roosevelt, *Strenuous Epigrams of Theodore Roosevelt.*

Chapter 2

1. Stories that begin this section are adapted from Edmund Morris, *The Rise of Theodore Roosevelt* (New York: Modern Library, 2001).

2. Ibid.

3. Theodore Roosevelt, *Strenuous Epigrams of Theodore Roosevelt* (New York: H.M. Caldwell, 1904).

4. Ibid.

5. Stories that begin this section are adapted from Carleton B. Case, *Good Stories about Roosevelt: The Humorous Side of a Great American* (Chicago: Shrewesbury, 1920).

6. Theodore Roosevelt, *The Great Adventure: Present-Day Studies in American Nationalism* (New York: Charles Scribner's Sons, 1919).

7. Ibid.

8. Stories that begin this section are adapted from John J. Leary Jr., *Talks with TR* (Boston: Houghton Mifflin, 1920).

9. Stories that begin this section are adapted from Paul F. Boller Jr., *Presidential Anecdotes* (New York: Oxford University Press, 1996).

10. Theodore Roosevelt, *American Ideals and Other Essays* (New York: G.P. Putnam's Sons, 1915).

11. Stories that begin this section are adapted from Edmund Morris, *Theodore Rex* (New York: Modern Library, 2001).

12. Theodore Roosevelt, *An Autobiography* (New York: Macmillan, 1913).

13. Roosevelt, *The Great Adventure.*

14. Frederick E. Drinker and Jay Henry Mowbray, eds., *Theodore Roosevelt: His Life and Work* (Washington, D.C.: National, 1919).

15. Stories that begin this section are adapted from William Roscoe Thayer, *Theodore Roosevelt: An Intimate Biography* (Boston: Houghton Mifflin, 1919) and Frederick Wood, *Roosevelt as We Knew Him* (Philadelphia: Winston, 1954).

16. Theodore Roosevelt, *The Strenuous Life: Essays and Addresses* (New York: Century, 1901).

17. Stories that begin this section are adapted from Drinker and Mowbray, *Theodore Roosevelt,* and Morris, *The Rise of Theodore Roosevelt.*

18. Stories that begin this section are adapted from Leary, *Talks with TR,* and Thayer, *Theodore Roosevelt.*

19. Roosevelt, *An Autobiography.*

20. Leary, *Talks with TR.*

21. Stories that begin this section are adapted from Morris, *The Rise of Theodore Roosevelt,* and a phone interview with Tweed Roosevelt, September 8, 2007.

22. Theodore Roosevelt, *America and the World War* (New York: Charles Scribner's Sons, 1915).

23. Theodore Roosevelt, *Realizable Ideals* (San Francisco: Whitaker & Ray-Wiggin, 1912).

24. Stories that begin this section are adapted from Leary, *Talks with TR.*

25. Stories that begin this section are adapted from Roosevelt, *An Autobiography.*

26. Roosevelt, *An Autobiography.*

27. Stories that begin this section are adapted from Wood, *Roosevelt as We Knew Him.*

28. Theodore Roosevelt, *Through the Brazilian Wilderness* (New York: Charles Scribner's Sons, 1914).

Chapter 3

1. Stories that begin this chapter are adapted from Edmund Morris, *The Rise of Theodore Roosevelt* (New York: Modern Library, 2001); and Frederick Wood, *Roosevelt as We Knew Him* (Philadelphia: Winston, 1954).

2. Theodore Roosevelt, *Through the Brazilian Wilderness* (New York: Charles Scribner's Sons, 1914).

3. Theodore Roosevelt, *The Foes of Our Household* (New York: George H. Doran, 1917).

Chapter 4

1. Stories that begin this section are adapted from Elting E. Morison, ed., *The Letters of Theodore Roosevelt*, 8 vols. (Cambridge, MA: Harvard University Press, 1951–1954); and Edmund Morris, *Theodore Rex* (New York: Modern Library, 2001).

2. Theodore Roosevelt, *American Ideals and Other Essays* (New York: G.P. Putnam's Sons, 1915).

3. Theodore Roosevelt, *Strenuous Epigrams of Theodore Roosevelt* (New York: H.M. Caldwell, 1904).

4. Frederick E. Drinker and Jay Henry Mowbray, eds., *Theodore Roosevelt: His Life and Work* (Washington, D.C.: National, 1919).

Chapter 5

1. Stories that begin this chapter are adapted from Edmund Morris, "Teddy Roosevelt," www.time.com/time/time100/leaders

/profile/troosevelt.html (accessed January 2008); and Theodore Roosevelt, *An Autobiography* (New York: Macmillan, 1913).

2. Theodore Roosevelt, *A Book-Lover's Holidays in the Open* (New York: Charles Scribner's Sons, 1916).

3. Theodore Roosevelt, *Outdoor Pastimes of an American Hunter* (New York: Charles Scribner's Sons, 1906).

Chapter 6

1. Stories that begin this chapter are adapted from Edmund Morris, *The Rise of Theodore Roosevelt* (New York: Modern Library, 2001).

2. Theodore Roosevelt, *The Strenuous Life: Essays and Addresses* (New York: Century, 1901).

3. James M. Strock, *Theodore Roosevelt on Leadership: Executive Lessons from the Bully Pulpit* (Roseville, CA: Prima/Forum Publishing, 2001).

4. Theodore Roosevelt, *Strenuous Epigrams of Theodore Roosevelt* (New York: H.M. Caldwell, 1904).

Chapter 7

1. Stories that begin this chapter are adapted from Edmund Morris, *The Rise of Theodore Roosevelt* (New York: Modern Library, 2001).

2. James M. Strock, *Theodore Roosevelt on Leadership: Executive Lessons from the Bully Pulpit* (Roseville, CA: Prima/Forum Publishing, 2001).

3. Albert Bushnell Hart and Herbert Ronald Ferleger, *Theodore Roosevelt Cyclopedia* (New York: Charles Scribner's Sons, 1941).

Chapter 8

1. Stories that begin this chapter are adapted from Boy Scouts of America, *Scouting: Ninth Annual Report* (New York: Boy Scouts of America, May 15, 1919); Frederick E. Drinker and Jay Henry Mowbray, eds., *Theodore Roosevelt: His Life and Work* (Washington, D.C.: National, 1919); Ferdinand Cowle Iglehart, *Theodore Roosevelt: The Man as I Knew Him* (New

York: Christian Herald, 1919); Daniel Jabe, "The Sons of the Nation: The Popular Appeal of the Boy Scouts of the Nation, 1910–1919," www.boyscoutstuff.com/text.html (accessed January 2008); William H. Kniffin, *Thirty Years of Scouting in Nassau* (Massapequa, New York: Theodore Roosevelt Council, Boy Scouts of America, 1999); William D. Murray, *The History of the Boy Scouts of America* (New York: Boy Scouts of America, 1937); Charles Hanson Towne, *Roosevelt as the Poets Saw Him: Tributes from the Singers of American and England to Theodore Roosevelt* (New York: Charles Scribner's Sons, 1923); and Frederick Wood, *Roosevelt as We Knew Him* (Philadelphia: Winston, 1954).

Appendix A

1. Boy Scouts of America. *Scouting: Ninth Annual Report.* (New York: Boy Scouts of America, May 15, 1919). Reprinted with permission.

Appendix B

1. Excerpt from an article by Theodore Roosevelt published in the May 1900 issue of *St. Nicholas* magazine.

Appendix C

1. Daniel Carter Beard Papers, Box 221 from the Library of Congress.

Roosevelt, newly tapped as vice presidential nominee for President
William McKinley, delivers a stump speech in Freeport, Illinois in
October 1900.

Roosevelt greets his former Rough Riders at a reunion in San
Antonio, Texas in April 1905.

Bibliography

Printed Sources

Anderson, H. Allen. *The Chief: Ernest Thompson Seton and the Changing West.* College Station: Texas A&M University Press, 1986.

Barrus, Clara. *The Life and Letters of John Burroughs.* 2 vols. Boston: Houghton Mifflin, 1925.

Beard, Daniel Carter. *The Autobiography of Dan Beard.* Library of Congress, draft.

Bishop, Joseph Bucklin, ed. *Theodore Roosevelt's Letters to His Children.* New York: Charles Scribner's Sons, 1919.

Boller, Paul F., Jr. *Presidential Anecdotes.* New York: Oxford University Press, 1996.

Boy Scouts of America. *Scouting: Ninth Annual Report.* New York: Boy Scouts of America, May 15, 1919.

Brands, H. W. *TR: The Last Romantic.* New York: Basic Books, 1997.

Case, Carleton B. *Good Stories about Roosevelt: The Humorous Side of a Great American.* Chicago: Shrewesbury, 1920.

Cordery, Stacy A. *Historic Photos of Theordore Roosevelt.* Nashville, TN: Turner, 2007.

Davidson, Donald J., ed. *The Wisdom of Theodore Roosevelt.* New York: Citadel Press, 2003.

Drinker, Frederick E., and Jay Henry Mowbray, eds. *Theodore Roosevelt: His Life and Work.* Washington, DC: National, 1919.

Hagedorn, Hermann, ed. *The Works of Theodore Roosevelt.* New York: Charles Scribner's Sons, 1926.

Hart, Albert Bushnell, and Herbert Ronald Ferleger. *Theodore Roosevelt Cyclopedia.* New York: Roosevelt Memorial Association, 1941.

Iglehart, Ferdinand Cowle. *Theodore Roosevelt: The Man as I Knew Him.* New York: Christian Herald, 1919.

Kniffin, William H. *Thirty Years of Scouting in Nassau.* Massapequa, New York: Theodore Roosevelt Council, Boy Scouts of America, 1999.

Leary, John J., Jr. *Talks with TR.* Boston: Houghton Mifflin, 1920.

McCullough, David. *Mornings on Horseback.* New York: Simon & Schuster, 1981.

Morison, Elting E., ed. *The Letters of Theodore Roosevelt.* 8 vols. Cambridge, MA: Harvard University Press, 1951–1954.

Morris, Edmund. *The Rise of Theodore Roosevelt.* New York: Modern Library, 2001.

————. *Theodore Rex*. New York: Modern Library, 2001.

Murray, William D. *The History of the Boy Scouts of America*. New York: Boy Scouts of America, 1937.

Robbins, Michelle, "Rooted in Memory," *American Forests*, March 22, 2003.

Roosevelt, Theodore. *African Game Trails: An Account of the African Wanderings of an American Hunter-Naturalist*. New York: Charles Scribner's Sons, 1910.

————. *America and the World War*. New York: Charles Scribner's Sons, 1915.

————. "The American Boy," *St. Nicholas*. May 1900.

————. *American Ideals and Other Essays*. New York: G.P. Putnam's Sons, 1897.

————. *An Autobiography*. New York: Macmillan, 1913.

————. *A Book-Lover's Holidays in the Open*. New York: Charles Scribner's Sons, 1916.

————. *Fear God and Take Your Own Part*. New York: George H. Doran, 1916.

————. *The Foes of Our Own Household*. New York: George H. Doran, 1917.

————. *The Great Adventure: Present-Day Studies in American Nationalism*. New York: Charles Scribner's Sons, 1919.

————. *Oliver Cromwell*. New York: Charles Scribner's Sons, 1900.

————. *Outdoor Pastimes of An American Hunter.* New York: Charles Scribuer's Sons, 1905.

————. *Realizable Ideals.* San Francisco: Whitaker & Ray-Wiggin, 1912.

————. *Strenuous Epigrams of Theodore Roosevelt.* New York: H.M. Caldwell, 1904.

————. *The Strenuous Life: Essays and Addresses.* New York: Century, 1901.

————. *Through the Brazilian Wilderness.* New York: Charles Scribner's Sons, 1914.

Strock, James M. "Theodore Roosevelt, Executive." *Theodore Roosevelt Association Journal,* Summer 2007.

————. *Theodore Roosevelt on Leadership: Executive Lessons from the Bully Pulpit.* Roseville, CA: Prima/ Forum Publishing, 2001.

Thayer, William Roscoe. *Theodore Roosevelt: An Intimate Biography.* Boston: Houghton Mifflin, 1919.

Towne, Charles Hanson. *Roosevelt as the Poets Saw Him: Tributes from the Singers of America and England to Theodore Roosevelt.* New York: Charles Scribner's Sons, 1923.

Wood, Frederick. *Roosevelt as We Knew Him.* Philadelphia: Winston, 1954.

Internet Resources

DeWan, George. "From Long Island to Over here." *Newsday,* 2007, < www.newsday.com/community/guide/ lihistory/ny-history-hs709a,0,7616454.story > (July 2007)

Jabe, Daniel. "The Sons of the Nation: The Popular Appeal of the Boy Scouts of the Nation, 1910–1919." Boy Scout Stuff Home Page, 1998, <www.boyscoutstuff.com/text.html> (January 2008).

Jenkinson, Clay S. "The Deep Authenticity of T.R." *Rough Rider Review,* May 2007, <www.medora.org/Utilities/Publications/rrreviewmay07.pdf> (July 2007).

Morris, Edmund. "Teddy Roosevelt." *The Time 100,* April 13, 1998, <www.time.com/time/time100/leaders/profile/troosevelt.html> (January 2008).

New York Times Archive, 1900–1919, <www.nytimes.com> (January 2008).

Theodore Roosevelt Association Home Page, 2007, <www.theodoreroosevelt.org> (February 2007).

Von Drehle, David. "The Myth About Boys." *Time,* July 26, 2007, <www.time.com/time/magazine/article/0,9171,1647452,00.html?cnn=yes> (July 2007).

Document and Photographic Archives

Brown Brothers, Sterling, PA

Library of Congress, Washington, D.C.

National Archives, Boy Scouts of America, Irving, TX

Raab Collection, Ardmore, PA

Ray H. Marr Collection, Dallas, TX

Theodore Roosevelt Collection, Harvard College Library, Cambridge, MA

Roosevelt acknowledges the crowd during his term as president around 1905.

Acknowledgments

I *want to acknowledge my debt* to a number of individuals for their comments, suggestions, and assistance. In particular, I am grateful to Toby and Tony Roosevelt for their help in the early stages of manuscript development and for introducing me to their cousin, Mr. Tweed Roosevelt, who offered some important corrections to the manuscript and authored the Foreword. I am also sincerely grateful to Mrs. Chandler Roosevelt Lindsley for her enthusiastic support during the final stages of manuscript development. Chief Scout Executive Robert Mazzuca of the Boy Scouts of America offered warm encouragement before starting this book, while David Harkins, David K. Park, and Richard Mathews reviewed the manuscript and cleared the use of the Boy Scouts of America's trademarks. Additionally, former Chief Scout Executive James L. Tarr offered kind words of approval. Wallace Finley Dailey, the curator of the Theodore Roosevelt Collection at Harvard, spent time locating most of the images in these pages. Thanks to Dr. Roger Schustereit, Mackie Kazdoy, Bob Reitz, Rex Lewis, Jeffrey English, Doug Traver, Bill Bliss, David D. Durrett, and Pat Bywaters, who read the manuscript and gave excellent advice on refining it. Dr. Robert Lee Edmonds's exceptional insight into the subject helped make this a much better book. I appreciate the assistance of Ray H. Marr, my Scoutmaster during the 1983 World Jamboree, who provided me with a copy of his annual Christmas card bearing our troop's picture taken in front of Mount Rushmore (I'm the lad in the back row directly beneath the gap between the heads of Jefferson and Roosevelt). I thank Ross Perot and his assistant Sandra Dotson for their help in this project along with the Honorable Pete Sessions and his wonderful staff members Meredith Lindsey, Flo Helton, and Patricia Pan. I also thank Judge Nathan E. White, Joe E. Harris, and Charlie Newcomer of the National Society of the Sons of the American Revolution, Steve Van Buskirk of the Veterans of Foreign Wars, Michael D. Buss of the American Legion, Carol Butler and Raymond A. Collins of Brown Brothers USA, and former Scout Executive H. M. "Smoky" Eggers for their enthusiastic support during the latter stages of manuscript development. Warm appreciation to Scout Executive Ponce Duran, Stan E. Allred and my other business partners, Jim Stevenson, Katherine Listi, and Randy Pennington for allowing me access to their vast network of associates, as well as to Joel Bozarth, the proprietor of *The Little Gym*, who graciously lent me working space each week in his facility to work on the manuscript while my children pursued athletics and martial arts. Thanks goes out to Jim Fair who offered his much-needed "attaboys" throughout every step of the development process; kudos to my production team including Alan Hebel, Ian Shimkoviak, Usana Shadday, Sharon Hodges,

ACKNOWLEDGMENTS

John Poole, Norma Olmos, and to Publications Development Company (PDC) including but not limited to Matthew Land, Nancy Marcus Land, Celeste Johns, and Elizabeth Chenette. Finally, I must thank my two editors, Brendan Murphy and Susanna Daniel, who helped me craft better sentences every step of the way.

Roosevelt delivers a speech from the train's platform around October 1907.

Photography and Illustration Credits

Theodore Roosevelt Collection, Harvard College Library: p. 1, p. 2, p. 20, p. 43, p. 44, p. 49, p. 50, p. 55, p. 56, p. 61, p. 73, p. 81, p. 83, p. 85, p. 95, p. 98, p. 112

Library of Congress: p. viii, Daniel Carter Beard Papers, Box 221; p. 19, cph3f06276; p. 62, cph3c31913; p. 67, cph3a40275; p. 68, cph3b11157; p. 74, cph3c31913; p. 105, cph3b2016; p. 106, cph3b43780; p. 116, cph3a44668

Ray H. Marr Collection: p. iv

David C. Scott Collection: p. xvii

About the Editor

A *lifelong Scout* and adult Scout leader, David C. Scott has been researching the emergence of the worldwide Scouting movement for the past decade. He has compiled a large archive of documents pertaining to the early history of Scouting and is an avid collector of original-edition books by the British and American founders of Scouting and related figures, as well as early handbooks and artifacts that he uses to illustrate his talks. He is a graduate of Vanderbilt University and holds a master's degree in applied economics from Southern Methodist University. Mr. Scott lives in Dallas with his wife, Aimee, and their four children.

The editor respectfully requests that any and all suggestions for changes and/or additions to the text for future editions be sent to:

ATTN: WAA Book
Red Honor Press
P.O. Box 166677
Irving, Texas 75016

WeAreAmericans@redhonor.com

About Red Honor Press

Red Honor Press is a special imprint of PenlandScott Publishers founded in 2006 for the ambitious purpose of uniting timeless, engaging, and enriching subjects and themes with outstanding authors creating distinctive titles for all ages and interests. Red Honor has quickly emerged as a resourceful publisher of quality educational, informative, inspirational books and media. The Press also produces award-winning and praiseworthy works for fraternal, faith-based, and service-oriented groups and organizations. The Red Honors mark of distinction—conceived by author and naturalist Ernest Thompson Seton—reflects the imagination and integrity underlying all Red Honor Press publications.

The eagle feather and three circles of brotherhood in the Red Honor Press colophon represent the commitment of the company to the ideals of Scouting and American values in business and in life.